Grace

Saved a wretch like me

By

Arylene Murphy

"To my Mum, who has always been there for me"

ISBN: 978-1-913275-19-8

This book was published in cooperation with
Choice Publishing, Drogheda, Co. Louth,
Republic of Ireland.
www.choicepublishing.ie

GRACE
Saved a wretch like me

Chapter 1

To the outside world as well as to my parents and siblings my childhood would have been considered to be perfectly normal, nothing especially different to that of my neighbours and friends – yet my memories of that time are centred around sexual abuse.

My recollections of *normal* significant events such as birthdays and Christmases are very vague. I do not remember my first communion or confirmation yet the image of being raped at the age of 7 on the kitchen floor of our family home is painfully vivid.

I am one of 6 children, second eldest, eldest girl, brought up in a typical home in a small town in Donegal. Although my parents were not overly demonstrative, we were very aware that we were loved and cared for. My Dad worked extremely hard to provide for his family and handed over his wage packet to my Mum, every week, unopened. With only one wage coming in, it must surely have been a constant struggle but we, as children were oblivious to that.

Our home was one of 20 terraced houses known proudly to those of us who lived there as the Rock. It was appropriately named as it loomed mountainously overlooking the town accessed only by a steep hill on one side and a stairway of stone steps on the other. Each house was inhabited by a young family or by an older couple with children almost reared. It was and still is, a street where neighbours helped each other out and children all played together.

1

We lived in No.12 which was on the straight stretch, a vantage point to get out of the way of traffic while playing Rounders. We seldom raced frantically to remove the makeshift markers as the traffic was more often than not Father Gibson visiting a parishioner or Eddie Frost transporting the bin collection to the local tip.

More frequent traffic was the construction vehicles coming and going from our own house, various shapes and sizes, painted orange with Carlton written on the side, the name of the company Dad worked for.

Carlton Construction was a family owned company, run by 3 brothers. The youngest of the three, Alan became Dad's closest friend and was to remain a very dear friend of the family for many years after Dad passed away.

As a young girl I always felt the need to be on the look-out, weighing up who to trust and being suspicious of most adults but Alan was one of the few people outside the family that I knew I was safe around.

A friend of mine at the time, Georgina lived at No.15 and her Dad worked for the E.S.B. (Electricity Supply Board) which meant he went to work in the morning and returned home in the evening. Our Dad worked away from home a lot and we usually only saw him at weekends.

Dad was very much 'an outdoors' man and loved to fish and hunt. We as kids, took turns to go with him either alone or in pairs though I always opted out of the shooting trips as I hated the guns. He would tell us stories of when he was young and that special time with him made up for the nights when he was away.

One great memory I have is of a particular Saturday morning when Dad was home and Mum had gone to Nora's, the hairdressers on the Port, to have her hair done. As school was closed, we had planned a game of Penalties, the girls against the boys with Dad in goal up in the Brothers field. Playing Penalties was so much better in the field than playing in the street because there were proper goal posts, but it had rained so heavily the night before that the area around the goal was too water-logged to play in.

"Why the long faces?" Dad asked with a wink.

Straight away we became excited as we suddenly realised, he had a plan of his own! Before he had an answer to his question, he had lifted an armchair and carried it out to the front garden!

"Grab an end", he said to my brothers Keith and Gavin as he came back in and reached for the couch.

When Mum arrived back from the hairdressers all the furniture from the front room was in the garden and we were playing Penalties inside the house.

My brothers and sisters often talk about other fun times we shared with Dad, but I have so few of those happy memories of my childhood as it was all shrouded by abuse.

When at home now we often take down the box of photographs that Mum keeps on top of the wardrobe in her room and go through the old school pictures. We all started school at about 4 years old in the Little Angels Primary School on the Rock, boys and girls up to age 7.

After making our First Communion the girls went to the Convent run by the Mercy nuns and the boys went to the De La Salle run by the Christian Brothers.

For the girls from the Rock that meant a long walk across town whereas the boys just hopped over the wall outside their front door because the boys' school was only yards away from where we lived. I was still in the Little

Angels when the abuse started.

My first distinct memory is of me lying on a damp grey blanket, the one Mum used as a draught excluder for the back door. A grown man was lying on top of me, his weight crushing me. I was terrified because I could not breathe. I thought I was going to die trapped beneath him.

Finally, he got up.

He took me by the hand and walked me into the front room. He pointed to the guns hanging on the wall over the 4 dining room chairs. I realised it was Saturday night because Mum had our Sunday clothes laid out on each chair. Keith's first, and then mine, and then Gavin's and last Michelle's. I fixated on the whiteness of the knee-socks on my mine.

"See them guns?" he asked as he shook me.

I nodded.

"If you tell, your Dad will shoot me, and he will go to prison forever. Your Mum will be left on her own with you kids and it will be your fault, right?"

He shook me again. I nodded again. I knew he was right.

The *Secrets* had begun.

I learned how to be silent in so many different ways. I would cry myself to sleep without making a sound, terrified that my sister Michelle, lying beside me would ask what was wrong. I would feel the tears running across my cheek and into my ear as I lay with my back to her pretending to be asleep. I would lie unmoving, rigid with fear and frantic with confusion and shame.

I knew I could not tell anyone but even if I could tell I did not know how. I did not know the words to explain it. I knew what had happened was wrong, but I could not understand why.

This initial event set the precedent for years of abuse and was the marker which determined the course of my adult life.

So many times, I wished that I could have told Mum, but fear prevented me. My youngest sister, Cathy was only a baby and the thought of Mum having to look after all 5 of us on her own as well as what it might be like for Dad if he had to go to prison petrified me. The threat from the man who abused me was very real and one that I was terrified of.

From that time on my childhood became a collection of images, snapshots of being abused with few glimpses of what childhood should have been.

Remembering in snapshots was my means of creating a personal history in a way I could manage but by filtering the memories in a way that I could cope with, I not only deleted parts of the details of the horror of the abuse, I also deleted parts of the joy of being a child.

I cherish the simple fond memories of being a little girl like when Georgina and her younger sister Denise would knock on our door for Michelle and me to go out to play Steps. This was a great game we made up which was simply bouncing a ball between the step on our side of the footpath and on Conlon's next door.

But every fond memory is tainted with one of abuse.

Mum had a friend who was away at college training to be a teacher but came home to her parent's house in Station Road on a regular basis. As it was long before the times when everyone had a phone Mum wrote a note and asked me to deliver it and wait for a reply.

It was a Sunday and I was wearing my good trouser suit instead of my usual play clothes. The suit was brown with a white stripe on the front, Michelle had one the same.

On the way back from the errand a white car pulled up along- side me. It was *him,* the man who had abused me. The passenger door opened, and he told me to get in. He drove up the road, away from the houses, stopped the car and sexually abused me. I started to cry.

"What are you whinging for?" he asked.

"My good trouser suit is all mess", I sobbed.

He came around to the passenger side of the car and told me to get out. He sat me down in the ditch and splashed up some of the muddy water on me.

"Tell your Mother that you were running, tripped and fell into the ditch and got your clothes wet", he said.

Mum was not too happy about me getting my good clothes dirty, but I was relieved that she believed the lie. So many times, I wish I could have told her the truth. She would have stopped it. But he was always around. His presence a constant reminder of the consequences for my family if I told. I became very quiet in the house, terrified that if I spoke at all, the secret would come out. I grew to be more frightened of telling than of the abuse itself.

The fear was over-whelming and I was frantic all the time. I knew I had to keep the secret!! I could never tell because if I did terrible things would happen to my family and it would be my fault. I was always on alert, hyper-vigilant and constantly aware of those around me and how I was interacting with them. I soon learned that it was easier and safer to just be on my own. This tactic created a new pain......loneliness. The loneliness and isolation seemed to reinforce the fear somehow, but it was the only way I knew to protect me from telling.

I remember one day being completely panic stricken when Mum passed an innocent remark. My older brother

Keith was asking me to play a game of table tennis with him.

"Come on Arl, just play one game", he pleaded.

"No", I replied adamantly. "I just want to be on my own".

Mum heard the exchange and commented, "There's our wee Greta".

She went on to explain that Greta Garbo was famous for using the phrase, *'I want to be Alone'* but the fact that Mum voiced her awareness of my behaviour frightened me so much that I suddenly jumped up to play the game.

Everything was so confusing. My behaviour was frequently commented upon after that but thankfully it became accepted as just being *my way*. I had my own spot at the corner of the red brick fireplace that Dad had built, and I would sit there of a night with my arms wrapped tightly around my knees, watching telly and biting my nails or chewing the inside of my cheeks. I frequently bit and pulled the skin from inside my mouth until I tasted blood.

I bit my nails until they too, were sore and bleeding. When I had bitten the nail down to the quick, I would bite the skin all around it. Dad tried many tactics to get me to stop biting my nails including duct taping my gloves on and applying foul tasting polish designed specifically to stop nail biting. He even offered me double pocket money for every individual nail I could grow! I tried really hard to do it but most times I was unaware of what I was doing and before I knew it the single nail that I had been tenderly nurturing was gone!

It was not always easy to hide how I felt because I often had no idea that my behaviour was out of the ordinary until it was pointed out. For example, going to see the Doctor was usually a drama. I had forgotten about these excursions until

Mum only recently recounted the stress of each visit to Doctor Quigley in the dispensary at the Rock Hospital when I had yet again complained of tummy ache.

The Doctor would obviously want to examine me, but I always kicked up a fuss. I would scream in protest when he tried to remove my clothes. With a lot of coaxing and encouragement from him and some scolding and bribing from Mum I would finally consent to being examined. He would have to put the stethoscope up under my clothes to listen to my chest and would struggle to get it down again because I was holding the edges of my jumper down so tightly.

These visits were a regular occurrence over the years but there was never a definitive diagnosis for the pain. I was tested for everything from constipation to appendicitis as well as every other disease and condition in between.

"I've a path beaten to this place Doctor," Mum would say.

"Packie and me are worried sick. Can't you find out what's wrong?"

I felt so guilty for making Mum and Dad worry so I stopped complaining.

I stayed quiet and tried to pretend that I did not exist.

I felt invisible and insignificant and always afraid.

In a strange sense this way of behaving grew to be less frightening because it was easier for me to keep the secret. All I had to do was to stay hidden, keep silent and pretend that nothing was going on.

My mistrust of adults outside of the family was reflected in my behaviour as was my hunger for the safe tactile affection from those within it.

Of a night-time I loved to sit on the floor beside Mum's chair and paint her long fingernails bright red. Of course, I would make an awful mess of them, but Mum would never let on. The varnish would be all over her fingers and put on so thickly that you could actually see the layers, yet Mum would hold up to the light as though to scrutinize them and then acknowledge the perfection of the job saying, "they are beautiful Arylene".

She obviously took it all off when I went to bed because the next day, they were talon perfect!

There was always so much to do during the long summer holidays from school when the weather was fine. On hot sunny weekdays Mum and Aunty Annie would bring us to the back of Thompsons, a safe and secluded beach in Portnason, where we would meet the O'Byrne's and other families from the area to spend all day swimming and playing on the sand dunes.

Other days we would meet with Mum's friend Mary Lee and she would bring us on a long walk up the Rock road. Mary was great fun and she always let us run ahead to pick blackberries from the bushes at the roadside.

One day as we passed a farmhouse a barking dog came running out and chased us. We dropped the berries as we ran back screaming with terror. Mary lifted a stick and shouted at the dog and it turned tail and ran home.

The only evidence of the berries was the staining on our mouths as we recounted the story to Mum when we got home.

On weekends, when Dad was home, we would drive to Rossnowlagh where the beach would be packed with people spending their holidays in the caravan parks and others would be visiting the Friary.

The best time of all was when Dad took time off work and we would go on special days out as a family. The photographs taken at Dublin Zoo and Westport House were proof of the childhood I wish I could remember better.

Going back to school after the long summer break was difficult but for those of us going into First class the year held a very significant event, First Communion. Throughout High Infants Sister Stella frequently referred to this momentous milestone but her reflection of it filled us with fear rather than relish. On the first Monday morning of the start of the school year, Sister Rose-Marion stood tall in her long black dress that reached the floor and had huge rosary beads dangling at her side from the belt buckled around her waist. She wore a long black veil attached to a white square covering her forehead and a big crucifix was perfectly positioned in the centre of a white bib as it hung from around her neck. Standing at the top of the class she waved a thin cane in front of her. We were to find out later that this weapon was known as *The Medicine Man*, which referred to the fact that you got your medicine if you misbehaved. It was difficult to fathom Sr. Rose-Marion's definition of misbehaving and maybe because of that *The Medicine Man* was a regular feature.

However, the sharp whack of it on the desk in front of you was usually enough to frighten the life out of you and you immediately got on with whatever task she had laid down.

"Bad girls and boys will <u>NOT</u> make their First Holy Communion!" she screeched.

Overwhelming fear gripped my heart and I felt it pound painfully in my chest as the tears flowed uncontrollably down my face and drop on to the tiny desk.

"She knows!" the voice in my head shouted frantically.

I jumped out of my skin when I heard her screaming my name…. Arylene Murphy, get out here", she roared as she yanked me by the arm and dragged me out in front of the class.

"You are disgusting a child!!", she bellowed as she whacked me across the back of the legs with the cane.

"Go home and tell your Mother not to send you back until you learn how to use the toilet".

It was only then I realised I had wet myself. The brand new, fire engine red tights that had looked so lovely that morning with my kilt with the pin in the front and my black patent shoes now had one leg soaked and smelling of pee.

I ran home across the Brother's field worried about what Mum might say but relieved to know that although Sr. Rose-Marion knew I was bad she did not know about the secret. When I got home, Mum stripped me off and stood me in the Belfast sink in the kitchen. The water was freezing until she topped it up with water from the kettle.

"Why didn't you tell the nun you needed the toilet?" Mum asked.

I did not answer.

I felt really safe as she wrapped me in the big bath towel and carried me into the armchair in front of the fire.

I started to cry.

"What's wrong Arylene?" Mum asked.

Still I did not answer.

I wanted to say something, but fear stopped me.

I have no recollection of my First Communion, but it was that same year I was admitted to the Rock hospital with pneumonia. I was in hospital for more than 4 months, but I have no memory of being in pain or feeling unwell. Although I was only 7 years old, I was in a ward with grown women and they spoiled me rotten.

There seemed to be no restriction on visiting as Mum was in and out at all times throughout the day, reassuring me that she was never too far away. The hospital was situated between the boys' school and the Little Angels and our house was only a stone's throw away but by now there was another baby in the family and yet Mum could always make time for visiting. My sister Cathy was born during the summer and how Mum managed is a mystery.

Dad came in at night and often brought Keith, Gavin and Michelle with him. Our Aunt Kate worked in the hospital so between all their comings and goings I did not feel at all homesick and for a time I was safe from the abuse.

The close proximity of the school meant that it was easy for Sister Rose-Marion to call in and I did not look forward to her visits. She came in to see me most evenings in order to correct the homework she had assigned the previous day and to leave me with work to do before her next visit.

My hospital stay went into the winter months and I awoke one morning to see thick snow piled on the window sill. When I looked outside, I noticed that there were no vehicles parked at the front of the hospital yet and a blanket of snow smoothly concealed the whole area.

Over the next few hours I watched as footprints and tire treads dented the thick covering and by mid-morning the whiteness of the snow had turned dirty brown with the busy traffic to and from the hospital. I could hear the children from the Little Angels and the De La Salle schools laughing and playing when they were let out for 11 o'clock break. I got upset because I could not go out to play in the snow with my friends. Sister Dolorous was one of the nursing nuns in the hospital and she tried to comfort me, but I would not settle.

"Wait a minute!" she said as she raced out of the ward and vanished.

I sat watching the door and wondered what was going on. I was beginning to question the likelihood of her return when she burst in carrying one of the big metal buckets used for rinsing the mops when the floors were being washed.

She tipped out the bucket in the middle of the ward and presented a pile of snow! With a big grin on her face she yelled to me,

"Come on then" as she stooped to grab a handful of snow.

I was hesitant about what to do because I felt sure that nuns did not play snowballs! I knew I was wrong when I felt the cold thud on the side of my head and with a squeal, I hopped out of bed to return the gesture. We played until the snow melted and Sister Dolorous had to mop up and return to duty.

I have no recollection of leaving hospital and going home.

I remember clearly the first time I went on holidays to Sligo. Apart from my stay in hospital Keith nor I had never been away from home before, so we were told if we felt homesick, we could come back whenever we wanted. We had often visited Aunty Teresa and Uncle Alec in Doorly Park, Sligo but had never stayed overnight and I was very excited as Mum packed our bags with enough clothes for a week.

On the morning of our departure we all clamoured into Dad's purple Anglia and set out on the 30-mile journey. When we arrived, Dad unloaded our bags from the boot and carried them into the house.

Our younger cousins were in the front garden playing football, so we all stayed outside as Mum and Dad went inside. We were all playing and chattering happily when finally, it was time for Mum and Dad to go home. Gavin and Michelle jumped into the back seat of the car and Dad got behind the wheel. Mum said she knew we were going to have a great time on our holidays but reassured us that we could come home if we wanted to. There was a yellow telephone box at the end of the road, outside Mrs. Tivlan's sweet shop and Mum told us that Aunty Teresa could ring Dad at work, and he could pick us up any evening on his way home if we were feeling homesick.

The first night lying in bed downstairs in the girls' room felt very strange. My cousin Teresa and I were sharing one of the double beds while the other was empty. Teresa's older sisters Kathleen and Trisha were out dancing at the local hop and would not be back until long after we would be asleep. I thought of Keith upstairs in the boys' room and wondered how he was feeling. Just then the door opened and young Alec, our cousin poked his head in and said,

"Who wants a biscuit?"

Teresa and I jumped out and snuck into the kitchen hot on the heels of Alec and Keith.

The house was in darkness and Alec went straight to the cupboard without bothering to turn a light on. He had obviously done this before as he had no problem navigating his way around the furniture without making a sound.

Everyone was in bed and it was thrilling to be creeping around as the household slept. Teresa opened the range door and the embers cast heat and light into the room. Alec was already buttering Marietta biscuits and laying them out on the table in two rows.

He then dipped one from each row butter-side down into the sugar bowl and laid it on top of the one on the opposite row. Suddenly we all froze as we heard the sitting room door creaked open! We were all in for a scolding if we had woken up Aunty Teresa or Uncle Alec.

"What are you lot up to?" It was Jimmy, one of the

younger boys.

"Give me one", he said.

Before long we were all tucking into Marietta sugared biscuits washed down with a mug of ice-cold milk and I did not feel at all homesick.

The next morning the house was a hub of activity. Uncle Alec and my older cousins were bustling about getting ready for work as Aunty Teresa buttered toast and poured mugs of tea. Even at this early hour Aunty Teresa was laughing and joking as she hurried the workers out the front door. She was always happy and had a warm, hearty laugh that was infectious. She seldom scolded but when she felt it was necessary, the cautionary reminder of 'Sally' was introduced.

'Sally' was the name given to the sally rod; a long, thin stick supposedly housed in the airing cupboard at the top of the stairs. As it was only ever used as a threat for punishment and never actually made an appearance, I doubted its very existence.

Aunty Teresa was always busy, whether it was up and down the stairs making beds, dusting and cleaning as she went or taking dry clothes from the line in the yard as she made room for the next load to hang out, it appeared as though she was constantly moving about the house. As she flitted from one place to another, she frequently stopped to check on whatever was boiling, roasting or baking in the White Aga in the living room.

The range was the centre of the home both literally and metaphorically as it not only cooked all the food but heated the water and warmed the whole of the house as well. The ability to use such a contraption was a very special skill as the fire had to be continually monitored, stoked and fed.

It would be burning from early morning and then

allowed to cool in the afternoon, only to be fired up again as Aunty Teresa prepared the evening meal.

There was always a lot to do around Doorly Park and one-day Jimmy said he was going to the 'Trolley Hill' and invited Keith and I to tag along.

"Put on your coats" Aunty Teresa said. "And stay away from the river".

The latter instruction was the one rule that we were constantly reminded of until we could chorus it along with her every-time we left the house. We never broke that rule as there were so much other activities to keep us busy.

Jimmy had his own home-made trolley as did the other kids at the Hill. None of the trolleys looked like expert pieces of machinery with two lengths of wood and scrap wheels nailed together being steered with string tied to the front. Only Aunty Teresa's prayers prevented serious injury as Jimmy took off from his pole position at the top of the hill to race to the bottom with his fellow speed junkies. Halfway down he lost control and crashed into the trolley on his left knocking them both into the ditch.

The other lad's trolley was undamaged, but Jimmy's did not fare so well. The big nail which held the steering on had been knocked loose. Jimmy looked around and found a makeshift hammer, a heavy rock which sufficed to carry out a roadside repair. He was back at the top of the hill ready for the next race. Keith and I cheered him on as he took off again, this time successfully crossing the winning line in one piece.

It was difficult for me to get to know the girls of my own age on the street and I discovered very quickly that they were not keen on playing on the 'Trolley Hill'. Although I desperately wanted to make friends, I was horribly shy and was more comfortable being with my cousins.

Trolley racing was considered to be more of a boy's past-time, but Keith and I had planned to make our own trolley using the wheels from the dolls pram that Santa brought me last Christmas as soon as we got home.

Kitty's Hill on the Rock would be perfect for trolley racing.

During dinner that evening I was so tired I was falling asleep at the table. Aunty Teresa announced it was nearly bedtime. The boys were objecting saying it was way too early when Kathleen and Trisha took out a record player. I quickly perked up. Everyone was singing but Alec stole the show.

♫ *"Knock three times on the ceiling if you want me, twice on the pipe if the answer is No-oo"*, ♫ he sang as he danced around the sitting room.

Although I loved being with my cousins, I was very self-conscious and more at ease when I was alone. Alec seemed to know that and always made a point of quietly talking rather than being boisterous and forcing me to join in. Alec was much older than me, yet he took the time and care to see that I was ok.

He was such a gentle soul and very kind-hearted, and I felt safe with him. It was not long before I was picking up the words and feeling confident enough to sing along to the chorus. It was to be another hour or more before I finally went to bed. I must have fallen asleep as soon as my head hit the pillow and I did not stir until the next morning.

Alec was waiting for me to get up, to give me a spin on the bar of his big black bicycle but I really wanted to learn how to ride it myself. He said he would teach me and would spend time of an evening when he finished work to take me out. On the first evening we went up and down the road until Aunty Teresa shouted for us to come in for dinner. We were starving and did not dally as we parked the bike in the front garden. I could already smell the mouth-watering waft of bacon, making my belly rumble with hunger. When we got in, I sat in my now usual spot at the table.

Aunty Teresa put my plate in front of me, boiled bacon with cabbage and mashed spuds. I quickly began to eat the bacon and spuds but left the cabbage untouched.

"Eat up that cabbage", Aunty Teresa told me.

"Yuk, I don't like it", I said.

"Well", she started. "If you eat up all your cabbage it will help you to ride the bike".

I tried a bit of the cabbage, but it tasted too awful.

When Aunty Teresa was busy getting dinner for everyone else, I scooped up the cabbage and tipped it out the open window beside me to the waiting cat sitting on the window ledge. The cat liked it and he soon cleared the lot.

I had an image in my head of the cat riding Alec's bike and chuckled to myself. That was to be the first of many holidays spent in Doorly Park where I eventually learned to ride the bike. Although I do believe I would have learned to ride a lot quicker if I had listened to Aunty Teresa and eaten the cabbage she cooked on a very regular basis.

I loved my time there and saw it as a haven. Not only did I feel safe from the abuse I also felt safe from the fear of telling. At home it was different.

I was always afraid ……. afraid of being abused and afraid that I would tell.

The only way I could survive was to imagine it was not so. It was like living in two places at the same time. I lived one inside my head and the other outside. When I looked at my friends, I knew I was different and wondered what it was like to be an ordinary kid. I wondered what it was like not to be afraid. I imagined living their life and struggled to picture what it would be like.

After learning to ride Alec's bike I was desperate to have one of my own. Being able to ride meant so much to me. It gave me a strange sense of freedom. It was something I was in control of. Mum said to wait and see, I might get one for Christmas. That seemed a very long way off and every night I asked God to please tell Santa to bring me a bike. As it was only September, I thought there was little point in pleading with Santa directly because he probably had not even started taking requests yet.

Finally, Christmas came and with it my blue Eska bike. My friend, Georgina got one too but hers was green. Together we would cycle for miles, up the Rock road or out the Knader Road towards the forestry. The best day of the week for a cycle was Sunday because there was nothing else going on in the afternoon.

After 11 o'clock Mass I would race home, across the Brother's field, to change out of my good clothes and go out again to play. It would not be long before Mum called us for dinner which was usually roast chicken with loads of roast spuds, peas and gravy.

Whoever finished first, more often than not, that was Gavin, would be given a big *tupperware* bowl to run to O'Neill's Shop at the Bridge End on the Port for Paddy's famous ice-cream. Mum would have a tin of fruit cocktail and some wafers to go with it. Sometimes, she would tell Gavin to get 99's, a chocolate flake for each of us, as an added treat.

One Sunday afternoon I called to Georgina's house to ask if she would come along for a cycle out the Knader Wood. Her Mum said that Georgina had a touch of a cold and because it was beginning to rain a little, thought it best that she stay indoors, in order to be fit for school the following day. I decided to go alone.

It was a long trek from the Rock, up to the top of the town and out past the Shiel Hospital but I did not mind. Once I got out past Falgarragh Park the long road towards the forestry was much quieter. As I got further out the road grew steeper and the surface less smooth, so it was difficult to cycle. It was at this point that Georgina and I would usually turn back but as I was alone, I decided to venture on a little further. There was very little traffic around, but suddenly I realised that a white car was slowing down alongside me.

My heart began to beat faster as I instantly realised who it was. I jumped off my bike and hastily turned it around in an attempt to go back the way I had come.

I heard the car stop and then he shouted,

"Hey Arylene", he said. "Hang on a minute".

I noticed that it was raining quite heavy by now.

He said, "Jump in the car and I'll run you home", as he reached to take hold of my bike. I held the handlebars tightly.

"Come on", he said. "Let go".

He lifted the bike into the back seat of the car and then opened the passenger door and waited as I got in. I watched him as he walked around the front of the car and got into the driver's seat.

"Have to go up the road a little bit", he said. "Just to turn around".

He drove for quite a while and although he kept talking, I never spoke. Finally, he pulled into a clearing but instead of turning, he stopped the car and turned off the engine. He continued to talk as he molested me, but I had 'tuned out' and did not hear what he was saying. I do not know if he threatened me again to prevent me from telling but I had

20

already learned that telling was not an option.

He dropped me off near the end of Falgarragh Park. I sat crying on the side of the road for what seemed to be a very long time. I do not know how long I sat there. I realised that it had stopped raining and it was beginning to get dark.

I thought that Mum would probably be looking for me by now to come in for my tea, so I got back on my back and headed for home.

I never went out the Knader without Georgina after that, but I would cycle to Rossnowlagh and just sit on the beach on my own. I loved Rossnowlagh, especially in winter when it was deserted. Sitting on a rock I could see for miles in every direction. Nobody could creep up on me.

Rather than feeling isolated I felt safe in the solitude. I found peace there. It was there I felt safe enough to allow the thoughts of the abuse come to mind. That was something I felt I had to do sometimes because the struggle of constantly pushing it all away would get too much. It was an ongoing battle, having to continually swap one thought for another. To have to always be aware of how I behaved or reacted was so tiring that I thought if I did not let some of it go the chances of my telling was a major risk.

That was a risk I could not take.

At first it was very frightening to allow myself to think about the abuse because I did not know if I would be able to put it all back, safely inside my head. Once I realised that it was possible to let some of it out and nothing terrible happened it became a way to lessen the burden. This was something that I just had to do as the abuse got more frequent.

I felt like I was living two lives in completely separate worlds - one was the world of doing the normal everyday things that kids do and the other was abuse and keeping secrets. It is difficult to comprehend how I managed especially when other adults became involved in the abuse but somehow, I was able to separate that and them from everything else.

The school day began with Michelle and I calling for Georgina and Denise and we all going down Kitty's Hill to call for Fionnula and Pauline on the Port. As a group we crossed The Bridge, climbed The Bank Bray and walked College Street to school in the morning and we all took the same track home in the evenings.

I could go to school, play with my friends and be at home with my family and never tell a soul about what was happening to me. I was able to be a typical kid when Rosie and her sister Laura and some of the other girls from the Rock included me in their games of House or Shop in the field behind Finnegan's house or when we all went across to the Brother's School to play Sevens. The De La Salle Brothers catered for boys of all ages with Primary School boys housed in one building and Secondary boys in the other.

Sevens was a game we played using a handball so the small alley between the two schools was ideal. We played in teams and on an evening after school or at weekends and holidays we rallied to pick up the score where we had left it in the last game.

One Sunday Michelle and I were excitedly discussing the plans to thrash the opposition as we were finishing the last of our dinner, when Mum announced it was Michelle's turn to help clear the table.

"You go on Arl" she said as she pulled the dinner plate from under Gavin's fork, "but keep me a place on your team".

As I rushed out the door, I heard Gavin shout, "Oi, I'm not finished me dinner yet!"

His second helping of roast potatoes and no promise of Paddy's ice-cream meant that he was not in his usual position of first to finish.

When I got to the school, I found no one else around the small handball alley so I thought I would have a few practice shots as I waited for Michelle and the others to arrive. I was completely engrossed in counting the unmissed shots when a tall figure dressed in black suddenly appeared beside me. I knew he was one of the Christian Brothers because although he wore a collar like a priest, he was wearing a long black frock down to his shoes.

"Hello", he said.

I was instantly frozen. I had never spoken to one of the Brothers before and Keith and Gavin were always saying how cross they were.

"What's your name?" he asked. He did not sound cross.

"Arylene Murphy", I replied shyly.

"Well Arylene", he said as he went down on his hunches to speak to me.

"Are you on your own?" he enquired.

"I'm waiting on the girls to play Sevens Brother".

I could not believe that I was speaking so much as I was usually so quiet and shy. It was probably because he was so friendly and not cross at all.

He suggested that everyone might be at the big handball alley on the other side of the Secondary school. He took me by the hand and led me around behind the school where he sexually abused me.

Then he said, "Don't tell anyone".

I never answered.

He was still adjusting his clothes as he walked away leaving me alone, terrified and confused.

23

I walked around to the front of the school and sat on the wall. I was trembling as I struggled to make sense of what had just happened.

He was a holy man! Now it was confirmed, I WAS bad. There was no other explanation. Whatever I was doing to make these awful things happen was the badness in me coming out. As I frantically rubbed away the tears before the girls came and started asking questions, I tried to think of something nice.

This often helped when I was lying in bed crying and worried about waking Michelle as she lay beside me.

I could see Aunty Annie's and Uncle Jake's house from the boys' school and wondered if we would be going to their house for supper tonight. They lived on the Steps side of the Rock and we loved going over there for Uncle Jake's black soup. The favour would be returned when our cousins came to our house on bath night. I was still thinking about the soup when Michelle and the others arrived.

Michelle excitedly shouted, "Come on girls! whose turn is it?"

Just then a terrifying thought struck me, *'one of them could hurt her!'*. From then on, I became more vigilant. I was thankful for the skills I had been teaching myself because now, they were going to be put to more important use and that was to protect my sister.

I knew that, unlike me Michelle was not bad, but I bet that I was bad enough for both of us. If anything happened to her it would be my fault, so I had to make sure that nobody could hurt her. The only way to make sure of that would be for me to stay away from her. My youngest sister, Cathy was still only a baby, so for now at least, I did not have to worry about having to protect her.

The summer had come around again and we all looked forward to the weeks off school and we discussed all the things we would do during the holidays. I was going to spend some of my holidays in Sligo, but Keith decided that he wanted to stay with his friends around home this year.

I could not wait to show Alec how good I had got on a bike and wondered if Aunty Teresa would still make me eat the cabbage even though I could now ride. I hoped they still had the cats just in case!

Going to Sligo for my summer holidays became an annual event but I always returned home for the last few weeks in order to settle and get ready for the beginning of another school year. This meant that I could catch up with my friends on the Rock and enjoy the last days of the holidays. Towards the end of the summer the boys' school would be open as the Brothers prepared for classes to resume. They would allow us kids from the Rock in to play but warned us not to damage anything.

One day, Brother Cillian from the primary part of the school gave each of the boys' two yellow dusters and told them to stand on each and slide up and down the corridor. It was not long before they had a great shine on the floor and the more it shone the faster they got. The girls were standing on the side lines cheering them on as they raced down to bounce off the wall at the end of the corridor.

Hide and Seek in and around the school was a popular past time for all of us. There were obviously loads of good places to hide. One Saturday morning we were playing in the building for the secondary boys and I was hiding under one of the tall benches in the science lab.

I heard the big, old wooden door creek open and I held my breath. I could hear someone creeping around and I stayed

25

frozen still with my eyes screwed shut hoping that I would not be found. Then a deep voice said in a whisper,

"Hello there."

It was the brother who had abused me. I tried to force myself further under the bench but there was nowhere to go.

"I've caught you" he said as he held his hand out.

"Come on out now," he said. "Don't be shy."

He reached in and in one movement he pulled me out and sat me up on the high bench. I kept looking at the door, praying that someone would walk in.

But it remained closed as he asked,

"What did you say your name was?"

I never spoke as he went on to molest me.

My early childhood was filled with reoccurring episodes of sexual abuse yet the incidents themselves were less frightening than the time between them. The constant fear of someone finding out was terrifying. Being afraid was a state that I knew well and in a crazy, contradictory way the fear was almost a comfort because it signified the preservation of the secrets. I had come to accept that being abused was something that I had no power over, I could not stop it or prevent it.

All I had to do was to keep it a secret. To do that I became a skilled liar. I was so ashamed because my lies protected the abusers and allowed them to do it again. I tried to avoid situations that would have given them an opportunity to molest me but that was very difficult as I tried to behave in a way that would not arouse suspicion.

I seemed to be always alert, always afraid, waiting for the monster to jump out of the dark. The darkness terrified me. I hated the winter evenings because darkness came too early and, so I would avoid going out again once I got home from school.

Occasionally though Mum would have to send one of us to Paddy's for a pint of milk if the 3 bottles left on the windowsill by Eddie McGarrigle that morning had been used over the course of the day.

Usually Keith or Gavin would immediately volunteer but sometimes, for one reason or another they would not be allowed to go e.g. Keith would have to do the homework that he was trying to duke out of, and Gavin would be grounded for his innocent but boisterous schoolboy antics.

That meant that I would have to go and because Michelle was too young there could be no argument.

There were two routes to Paddy's from the Rock, the steps and the hill. Either option evoked instant terror because there were so many dark corners and numerous hiding places. I reasoned that running down the hill and up the steps was the quickest and less hazardous way of doing it.

If Mrs. Finnegan had her hall light on it would not be so bad running down the hill but there was no such reprieve possible for the race back up the steps. Getting a tight grip on the carton of milk I would take a deep breath at the bottom of the first flight of steps and run, up the second flight and then the third and last before coming to level ground. Having climbed the three flights, the shortest but most petrifying part of the journey was still to be endured.

The flicker of a lit cigarette from a dark corner or the rustle of movement from behind the low wall would make my heart stop. Sometimes I would be able to take another breath and continue to run but other times I would be literally paralyzed with fear, frozen and unable to move. I never understood how the same situation could elicit two opposing reactions, but I knew that I had no power over it. There was no way of predicting whether the person with the cigarette or the movement behind the wall posed a risk or not. I could not find sense or rational as the intense fear generated within me was always the same and outside of my control.

Journeying up and down the Rock would not hold the same fear during day light hours and because of that I would often stand at the top of the steps looking out over my hometown. The big town clock dominated the landscape, with Saint Ann's church to the left and the Mercy convent to the right.

Looking down was a long drop into Sweeny's yard. I would contemplate the fall over. Toying with the possibility of dying gave me an immediate sense of relief but this was short-lived as I considered the consequences of not dying. There would no doubt be endless questions as to how and why I came to be up on such a dangerous ledge. I would not have been able to answer those questions because how could I explain why I wanted to die.

Although I have very few good memories of my childhood, I do have a genuine awareness of the kindness of the two lay teachers in St. Catherine's National School, one who taught 2nd class and the other 4th class. Mother Michaela taught 3rd and like Sister Rose-Marion she ruled with the assistance of a long thin cane though past experience had conditioned us all to be wary and the need for its use was therefore less.

However, that more or less depended on the humour of Mother Michaela than on whether we misbehaved or not.

Sister Eugenia who taught us 5th and 6th class, on the other hand did not need any such tool to put the fear of God into us. She terrified us all.

Chapter 2

After completing national school, I moved up to the secondary school. I was 11 years old. Although the secondary school was on the same ground as St. Catherine's it was called The Sacred Heart and was much bigger as it housed almost 400 hundred students. There was a boarding school attached which meant that girls from far and wide could attend. Secondary school was very different and was nothing like what we had previously experienced. I found it very daunting at first but soon got on with it. I made life-long friends throughout my school years and am so grateful for the support they knowingly and unknowingly gave me.

Most of the friends I had in St. Catherine's also moved up to The Sacred Heart. We were all so relieved to be getting away from the terrifying Sr. Eugenia that nothing imaginable could have daunted us.

Sister Jennifer, the Head of the Secondary was said to be very formidable, but we all thought nothing could have been as bad as what we were leaving.

She had earned herself the reputation of not only being very strict but of being very fair. We all looked forward to this new experience.

Secondary school was different in that, rather than having one teacher for all subjects we had a different teacher for each subject. This was great for me because it made it much easier to *hide*. I was an over-all average student. I did not stand out in any way. Being average meant that I was part of the majority and could blend in.

For the first time I had a school uniform and unlike most of the students I was really excited about that. Suddenly I became invisible, insignificant and safe. We all wore bottle green knee length skirts and V-neck jumpers, with a white shirt and red tie. For cold wet days we had a long gabardine coat and a smart blazer for milder days.

A few of my friends fought to hang on to their individuality and adjusted the uniform in subtle ways for example by rolling the waistband of the skirt in order to shorten it or loosening the knot on the tie to leave it askew, a habit that

Sr. Jennifer was determined to stamp out. It was to be a forever losing battle on her part. There was also a strict regulation around the wearing of 'indoor shoes.'

Not changing from outdoor into indoor shoes was a behaviour most of us indulged in. In some cases, including my own for the simple reason we only had one pair of good shoes.

There were frequent but irregular checks for indoor shoes. The only warning a whisper "Jenny's on the warpath! Jenny's on the warpath!" which would reverberate throughout the school at 2 minutes to 9 o'clock just before the first class of the day was due to start.

Then there would be an immediate scramble to get back to the cloakroom to retrieve the hideous slippers some of us had for such an event.

The fear of being caught with outdoor shoes on sometimes meant that all integrity was forgotten, and every girl was out to save herself!

One such morning the race was on but when my friend Mary got to her slipper- bag she found it empty. She had no choice but to keep her wet shoes on and just pray that Sr. Jennifer would not inspect our French class. It was not to be.

Sr. Jennifer walked in and we all stood up. I looked over at Mary and saw the panic on her face. Eileen was standing beside her and looking strangely confident.

Eileen seldom had indoor shoes, slippers or otherwise and was always being kept back for evening study for breaking the rules. Sr. Jenifer paraded us up to the front of the class, one by one to check our shoes. When it was Eileen's turn everyone was surprised to see her with a very dry pair of brand new Brogues.

But they were not hers, they belonged to Mary!

As Sr. Jennifer worked her way down the line the fear on Mary's face became more apparent as she looked down and saw the very obvious discolouration of the brown leather on the toe of her shoe caused by walking into school that morning in the rain.

"Mary Keenaghan, step forward please", Sr. Jenifer said rather quietly although it was a demand, not a request.

Everyone knew you were in trouble when any of the nuns used your surname!

"Have you changed your shoes?" Sr. Jennifer asked even though she already knew the answer.

"No Sister", Mary replied. "Someone stole my shoes Sister".

"What?" Sr. Jennifer roared, "Is it not more likely that you have mislaid them?"

To insinuate that there might be a thief in the <u>convent</u> school was a bigger crime than breaking any of the rules.

"Yes Sister", Mary answered, all the while looking straight ahead rather than indicate that someone actually had stolen her shoes.

Mary got an extra hour evening study as punishment and for once Eileen was not on Sr. Jennifer's hit list. Friendship only went so far though and Eileen had to buy Mary a bag of Tayto from the Tuck shop, every 11 o'clock break for a week.

My adolescence was very confusing because in some ways I wanted to be acknowledged yet I was terrified of being noticed. I was very introverted, and I envied the freedom my friends seemed to have had, just to be themselves. I had absolutely no sense of who I was or where I fitted into the world. I felt like a spectator, always on the outside looking in and never being a part of things.

I pretended to like the things my friends liked so that I could pass myself off as 'normal'. I desperately wanted to be normal, but I knew that I was not. I felt such a fake and always felt guilty for putting on an act. When we got together to question and giggle about the mechanics of sex like all schoolgirls would, I was very aware that I knew more than the others, but I would lie just to be the same as them.

I did not dislike or disagree with what my friends were *into* at the time e.g. their favourite bands like Meatloaf or Pink Floyd or popular T.V. shows like Mash or Dallas - I just did not know whether I liked those things or not. I felt the same about having boyfriends even though I had posters of David Essex and Leo Sayer hanging on my bedroom wall, which I had carefully removed from the centre pages of Jackie or Blue Jeans. All of this seemed strange to me as I came to realise that I had no real identity. I knew who my family were and where I came from, but I had no idea about who I was or who I was supposed to be.

I knew I was not like my friends and could not fully connect with what was important to them. There seemed to be a never-ending abyss between their world and mine. I felt detached and very lonely.

By now I was deliberately hurting myself. I started by slapping myself, anywhere on my body and progressing to hitting myself hard enough to leave a bruise. I became very self-conscious of the bruises and was worried about being asked how I had gotten them, so I started sticking needles in myself instead. I always kept a needle in the tin box we all had for our geometry set for school. I did not really know why I was doing these things except that it made me feel differently, at least for a short while. I felt less alone.

Had I shared my true feelings, my friends would have been amazed because they saw me as one of them, an active member of our exclusive group.

We were the group who broke the very strict rule of not leaving the premises during school hours. We were the ones who went to Duffy's shop to buy cigarettes at 5pence each and went down the convent grounds to smoke during break times. This crime was a legacy, handed down from past students and was therefore known by the powers that be, and so a member of staff was posted to prevent such antics. The job was, more often than not, given to Mr. McGlinn. Whether that was due to his speed and agility or in reference to the fact that he himself was a smoker, known to all the students as 'Smokey Joe,' I do not know.

Whatever the reasoning, it meant that we had to have a regular 'look out'. Whoever was assigned this important task took it very seriously as the safety of the group depended on the ability to disperse in seconds. As partners in crime we developed a bond as we entrusted the quality of our future time under the regime of Sr. Jennifer to one another.

By the time I was 14 years old I had been abused by 8 different men, but what I struggled most with was that one of my abusers was a woman. Somehow it was worse that a woman could sexually abuse a child.

Up to that time I had come to accept that abuse was part

of my childhood and I was learning tactics about how to try to keep myself safe from men. Being in the company of women meant I could let my guard down for a while. I did not have to be on alert and judge my every move.

Being abused by a woman destroyed my whole world view and any hope that I felt I might have had for some kind of peace in the future. She damaged me in ways the male abusers did not because it was betrayal at a much deeper level.

I could not process or come to any kind of understanding about how a woman could sexually abuse a child and therefore I could not put it away in the same place that I put all the other stuff.

It was only the ability to dissociate from the abuse itself that enabled me to function in any way at all, but I found it impossible to manage the effects of what she had done. My world was completely shattered, and I was terrified when I felt that I had run out of ways of trying to cope.

It was at this stage that I developed a problem with food. Having to eat became an enormous issue. I avoided eating whenever I could. I frequently told Mum that I had dinner in Georgina's or in another friend's house and although I felt guilty about lying, I also felt in control somehow.

This sense of control was very short lived though, because hunger would get the better of me and I would be forced to eat. I felt so angry and disgusted with myself when I had to give in to the pangs of hunger.

For the first time I seriously thought that maybe I could tell Mum, at least some part of what had been happening to me. I felt like a pressure cooker with all the steam building up, waiting to explode. Contemplating telling anyone about all the abuse was too overwhelming but maybe just letting a little of the steam out would ease the pressure.

The first person to abuse me had left to go to work in England and no one seemed to know exactly where he was. I felt it would be safer to tell Mum about him as he was no longer around and the threat that he made was less likely to become a reality. Maybe telling mum would create a space that would allow me to get some kind of peace in my head.

I spent weeks worrying about what might happen if I told but finally, I knew that I could not manage on my own any longer. Mum and I often sat up late when Dad and the others went to bed. I figured that this would be an ideal time to finally speak up.

"Mum", I said. "I need to tell you something, but you have to promise not to tell Dad".

Her face was instantly worried, but she replied "Arylene you know you're Father and I talk about everything, especially you lot."

"Mum please, I have to tell you something, but I can't if you don't promise." I wailed.

She suddenly realised how serious I was and eventually said, "I can't promise I won't tell your Father, but I promise to do what is best for you, is that fair enough?"

I was not entirely happy about this but sensed that it was as far as she would go. As well as that I trusted her to do what was right for us all.

Now that I had begun, I suddenly froze and could not speak. I had practiced what I would say and played it through in my mind many times over the past weeks but now I seemed to be struck dumb. I was absolutely terrified and my whole body began to shake.

Mum looked really scared and said, "Jesus, will you tell me what's wrong?" as she came over to sit beside me on the couch and held my hand.

And finally, I told her. It was 1978 and I was 14 years old.

We sat till the early hours as I spoke, for the very first time about how I was sexually abused by the man who was now working somewhere in England. She was distraught and devastated that I did not tell her at the time so that she could have protected me. Telling Mum gave me immense relief and although I had only told her a fraction of the abuse, I felt that a weight had been lifted. For so long I had to handle it all on my own but now Mum was with me to help me to carry the load.

Every now and again I would suddenly panic and feel sick with fear simply because I had dared to voice this massive secret. I knew that I could trust Mum but the fear I had been carrying for years still had a hold of me. I knew if Dad found out nothing would stop him from travelling to the ends of the earth to find this man and do exactly what had been predicted.

The threat I received as a seven-year-old was still as real as it had been then.

For so long I had been keeping the secrets and the awareness of having told sometimes gripped me and terrified me. This somehow added to the fear as I trusted myself less. Mum reassured me by promising not to tell Dad as she too believed as I did, that he would do something which we would all regret. Because Mum believed that I was no longer in any kind of danger, as the man I told her about was no longer in the country and I had not told her about any of the others, she was completely oblivious to the fact that I was still struggling.

By now a number of my early abusers seemed to be no longer around. At the time I had no idea if they had moved away or if, for whatever reason, they just stopped abusing me. The woman had also stopped molesting me, because she no longer had access to me, but I would come in contact with her on a regular basis. Just being in her presence made me feel powerless and afraid. I felt ashamed and confused that I could not tell anyone, not even my Mum about what she had done.

I believed that all the people who had abused me, did so because they saw something in me – something that I was doing wrong. It tortured me as I desperately tried to figure out what it was that they could see.

It was as though I was giving off a signal which gave them permission to abuse me. I hated myself for doing that but because I had no idea what I was doing wrong I felt utterly powerless and pathetic. The more I thought about it the more guilty and ashamed I would feel.

I hated myself on the inside and I hated myself on the outside too. Every time I had to look in the mirror, I was disgusted with what I saw, so I avoided looking. When washing my face or brushing my teeth I kept my head down in the basin and turned my back when brushing my hair. I cut most of my hair off on a number of occasions and was brought to Una's hairdressers at the bottom of the steps in an attempt at some kind of rescue, but it was usually beyond saving.

One of my teachers in Secondary School was Sister Sheila and for some reason that I could not grasp, she took an interest in me and I instantly trusted her. That was unusual as I was primed to be wary of most adults especially those that I did not know well but something inside me told me that I had no need to be cautious of this kind, gentle woman. Sister

Sheila encouraged me to join the choir and I loved it. I never missed a practice.

One day she asked me to stay behind to help her collect the hymn books. That day was to be the beginning of a lifelong friendship that only she and I really understood. At the time my classmates found it incredulous that I would be close to one of our teachers. I could not explain it to them because I did not really understand it myself. That time a student did not speak to a nun unless spoken to first.

Even then the only response we were advised to make was, 'Yes Sister' or 'No Sister'. Anything further would be considered insolence and immediate punishment meted out.

Sr. Sheila was to remain my friend even when my life was to continually take a downward spiral as I got older. She was my one constant and I trusted her with my soul. Given her way of life she was certainly well qualified for that job, but it was who she was as a human being that allowed me to share my feelings.

She was so easy to talk to and I felt some sense of being 'normal' when I was around her. Somehow, she just knew that there was something terribly wrong, but she never pressured me to talk about anything I was uncomfortable with. I loved and respected her so much for allowing me to do that.

I was an adult before she became aware of the full extent of the abuse. For many years I felt that I was on the outside looking in and Sr. Sheila made me feel less alone. I frequently spent hours with her in one of the parlour rooms in the big Mercy Convent beside the school and I am in no doubt that I would not have survived without her. I would never have been able to tell her all of the horror of the abuse because I was unable to process it all myself but when we talked I was able to share little pieces at a time, just enough to lift off some of the terrible weight I felt.

I became such a regular visitor to the convent that before long I was no longer considered a visitor that had to request entry by the official front door, I had instant access to the small side door.

Soon, even the non-teaching nuns knew me by name and often invited me to eat with them in the big refectory or to join them in evening prayer. For me, it was a huge honour to be a part of their very private lives. I felt an immediate and ongoing sense of safety and peace while in the convent and it was inevitable that I would want to remain in that environment. I never told my school friends about this because I was still doing my best to blend in and not to stand out. I told Sr. Sheila that I wanted to enter the Mercy Order as a postulant.

Soon after I told my parents and my family of my intentions and no one was surprised by the choice I had made. Mum and Dad would support me in whatever I needed to do to be happy although Dad did suggest *"that there were plenty of other things I could do!"*

Sr. Sheila made arrangements for me to visit a Mercy house in County Tyrone and I was very excited though anxious, when the planned day finally arrived. The car journey seemed very long as I sat in the back seat of the yellow and blue mini clubman Dad drove and it was undoubtedly further lengthened by his disapproving silence.

Mum sat in the passenger seat and continually turned around to reassure me by saying that I did not have to make any definitive commitment on that day as it was merely a meeting in order to speak with the Mother Superior. That was to be the first of many visits and weekend stays as I contemplated spending the rest of my life as a Mercy sister.

Before I could do that, I had to finish secondary school. I was in my final year and preparing for my Leaving Cert Examination.

As seniors we had more opportunities for extra-curricular activities, and some took us outside the confines of the school grounds e.g. debating bouts against other schools. As convent girls we were expected to behave in a certain way, and it was this exact expectation that encouraged some of us to misbehave.

The majority of the behaviour would have been considered by most to be misdemeanours and although a report of an overt expression of school-girl garishness would be frowned upon, it would not warrant a punishment. However, sometimes the behaviour would go beyond that and the antics during a trip to Ards friary was a prime example.

It was decided that those who wanted to could go to the monastery of Franciscan monks on the Donegal coast at Creeslough for a weekend retreat. Going away as a group was very exciting and we were all looking forward it. Sr. Christine and Sr. Baptiste taught us religious instruction and they, with two of the younger nuns would be coming with us. We were told, in no uncertain terms, that we were not going on holiday. It was a religious retreat and all of our time would be taken up with prayer, reflection and spiritual guidance.

Of course, a few of the girls had other ideas!

When we arrived at the monastery on the Friday evening, it was immediately obvious that there was something special about the place. It was so quiet and serene that you could not help but feel a sense of peace around you. The monks welcomed us with joviality which surprised us as we expected them to be pious and staid. The first night was fantastic fun as Brother Pascal entertained us with his piano playing and we all sang along to his rendition of ♫"If I were a rich man"♫

One of the younger nuns who came with us brought a guitar and finished the proceedings with John Lennon's, ♫ Let it Be ♫. As we listened the group instantly fell to a calm silence. 11pm was bedtime and we were all directed to our rooms.

In some rooms there were three beds, others four and although we were tired, we tip-toed to one another's rooms until the early hours, whispering and chatting about how surprising it was that a religious retreat could be so much craic.

The knock on the door by the heavy fisted Sr. Christine came far too quickly and we were all a lot less lively as we queued for breakfast in the refectory the following morning.

It was Saturday and it was down to serious business. The day was entirely filled with what we had been told a retreat was all about i.e. a lot of praying and reflecting although we did manage to sneak in a smoke once or twice. By evening we were all exhausted and it was apparent that some got more from the day than others. There was to be no entertainment that night as bedtime was at 9.30pm in preparation for Mass with all the monks early the following morning. However, some of the girls had planned their own entertainment.

The word went around that everyone was meeting in Room 1, the one furthest away from the nuns in Room 12. I really did not want to go but I did not have the confidence to speak out. I somehow knew that, whatever had been planned would be serious and I did not want to get into trouble. It meant a lot to me to be included in my friends exploits as it reinforced my acceptance from the group, but I was also very afraid of attracting any kind of attention to myself.

Everyone waited for the building to fall into silence and then crept along the corridor to tap gently on the door of Room 1.

One of the older girls had smuggled in a nagin of Vodka, which is the smallest size bottle you can get. When I was handed the glass with the vodka in it, I took a very small sip. It burned my throat and it tasted awful as it was diluted with water rather than with a mixer like coke or red lemonade.

There was not enough alcohol to get anyone drunk but the seriousness of what we were doing put us all on a high. The last night of the retreat went out with an act of rebellion rather than with a prayer!

Our wake-up call the following morning was not the heavy thump of Sr. Christine but a frantic rapping on the door by Sr. Baptiste.

"Hurry up you lot!" she shouted in panic.

"We have all slept late and when I find out who did it there will be wigs on the green, let me tell you!"

We found out later that drinking was not the final act of rebellion of our weekend retreat....

At some time during the early hours when the nuns were sound asleep, someone crept into their room and took the batteries out of their alarm clock. No one ever admitted to the brave, if foolhardy deed.

Back at school the following Monday morning there was a 'different' kind of quiet in the assembly hall. Everyone stood stock still in the appropriate row for their year. First years stood at the front, Second years behind them. Then the Inter

Certs, and behind them the Fifth years. We as Leaving Certs stood at the back.

Sr. Jennifer assumed her usual position and posture on the stage, looking into the middle-ground. Her face was, in this arena, usually expressionless, but on this occasion, there was no attempt on her part to hide the boiling point temperature of the blood cursing through her veins. That was likely to be the only location of heat as the hall had a frosty and chilling atmosphere. She held her hands behind her back, but no one was in any doubt that her fists were clenched and her knuckles white. She stood there for what seemed like an eternity, as teachers and students waited for an explosion that did not come.

Finally, she spoke. It was almost a whisper but could be easily heard by those of us at the back of the hall as was her intention.

"Brother Francis telephoned me," she said. "From Ards".

We froze. The entire assembly was unmoving.

A few of the First years, who were not yet familiar with the protocol required for such an occasion began to fidget. The icy glare from Sr. Jennifer was enough to return them to stillness. She resumed her dialogue.

"To inform me that he had found an empty nagin of Vodka in the bin in the kitchen".

"Will the girls who disrespected the sanctity of the retreat, please come up here?"

It was not a request, but a command.

"Now!" was her final word.

No one moved.

The tension in the air was suffocating. I could hear the rapid rate of my own heartbeat and felt a choking sensation in my throat.

I was terrified that I would cough. Then I heard a giggle!

At first, I actually thought it was me but then realised it was coming from the person beside me…Eileen.

"Shush!" I said out of the corner of my mouth, but it was too late.

Eileen was trying desperately to be quiet, but she could not stifle the nervous giggle. With an inhale of breath, she let out a deafening snort which reverberated around the assembly hall.

"Eileen Hogan!" Sr. Jennifer bellowed. "Come up here!"

Eileen slowly began to move and with her head down she sauntered up through the rows of students to the stage. It was clear to see that she was still giggling as her shoulders shook with each step she took. It was obvious that Sr. Jennifer was furious as she stood ramrod still with her clenched fists now held tightly by her sides. We all feared what would happen as Eileen stood in front of her.

"Were you drinking when you were supposed to be on retreat?" Sr. Jennifer asked.

The hall was deathly silent as everyone watched the uncomfortable exchange.

"No Sister" Eileen replied.

"Who brought the alcohol?" Sr. Jennifer enquired although she was likely to have been anticipating the response.

"I don't know Sister" Eileen said.

Sr. Jennifer then asked. "Did you take the batteries out of Sr. Christine's clock?"

Before Eileen could answer the hall erupted in laughter. Even the teachers were trying to hide their mirth including Sr. Christine.

Sr. Jennifer was certainly not amused and with an authoritative wave of the still clenched fist she dismissed the assembly and ordered everyone to class.

"Not the girls who were on retreat!" she shouted over the bustle of everyone's needing to escape.

We hung back and waited to hear our fate.

Sr. Jennifer questioned each of us but there was, of course the individual and collective response of innocence and ignorance. As it was only a few weeks before the beginning of our Leaving Cert exams we were possibly less terrified than if we were not due to be finishing school in the near future.

However, none of us were entirely naive about how difficult Sr. Jennifer could make our final school days and even with that thought in mind we each remained 'tight lipped' as our group solidarity was challenged, for what was likely to be the last time.

Eventually, defeated and frustrated, Sr. Jennifer delivered our punishment. As day students our school day usually finished at 4pm but we were ordered to return every evening at 6pm to study with the borders up to 9pm, until the exams were over. As well as that we were not allowed to attend the Debs Dance although with only about a week to go before the event, that ban was lifted.

Maybe the possibility of any lifelong, damaging effects on any of us swayed Sr. Jennifer into changing her mind about the dance.

Attending night study turned out to be a blessing for me as it was so much easier to prepare for the exams than trying to study among all the activity going on at home. There were no distractions in night study, and it was always supervised by one of the nuns.

Once the last exam was over, we all thought of little else

other than the results. Most of the students worried about getting enough points to get into the college or university they had chosen, or for getting a job with the Bank or the Guards but for me, it was just about achieving something, not being a failure.

My friend, Rosie from the Rock, had done her Leaving Cert a couple of years ahead of me and it was she who got me through those weeks of waiting. We would spend most weekends driving around in her little green car during the day, going to Rossnowlagh or Mullaghmore beaches and then going to the Hollyrood Hotel in Bundoran or the Melvin Bar in Kinlough at night. Rosie never drank alcohol and I was still underage, but we loved going to listen to the music and soaking up the atmosphere of the crowd.

Finally, before the end of the summer I was sitting in Sr. Jennifer's office.

As she sat behind her desk in the eerie silence of the still empty school, her expression was unreadable as she scrutinized the papers in front of her. I was sick with fear and apprehension, as I sat wringing my hands in my lap and trying hard to just keep breathing.

After what seemed like an age, she handed me a sheet of paper. I looked down the list of subjects with the grade marked alongside each. When I finished, I looked from the top to the bottom again, hardly daring to believe that I had passed! I checked again but yes; I had definitely passed!

I had passed school exams before, I even did well in the Inter Cert Exam but this, the Leaving Cert, was the big one! I was 'over-the-moon'. Even Sr. Jennifer's comment about I could have done better did not dampen my excitement.

"Yes Sister, thank you Sister" I replied cheerily as I raced out of her office.

Rosie was sitting in her car, outside the school gates waiting for me. The speed with which I ran while waving the piece of paper was an indication of how I had done but my high-pitched shout of 'I passed' certainly put to right her wondering about my success.

"Good on ya!" she exclaimed as I jumped into the passenger seat.

As Rosie drove me through the town and home to the Rock, she tooted the car horn all the way like cars do at a wedding. I hung out the window to shout and cheer with the other leaving certs from The Sacred Heart, The De LaSalle and The Vocational School, who were all celebrating their results. When we got to the Rock and stopped at our house, I could see Mum standing at the window, waiting anxiously for me. In an instant she knew the news was good and as she came running out, I was suddenly aware of something that I had never felt before, pride.

For the first time in my life, I was proud of myself.

"Told ya Lough Derg would do it!" Rosie said as she slapped me on the back.

"Yeah, you were right" I said.

The week before Rosie had convinced me to do the notoriously laborious three-day pilgrimage to the famous island, situated near Pettigo between Donegal and Fermanagh. The pilgrimage involved 3 days of fasting while walking and kneeling on rocky 'stations' barefooted as well as an all-night vigil in the Basilica. Although it was summer it rained continuously and the wind blowing around the small island made it very cold, especially as we were without socks or shoes.

The island is also known as Saint Patrick's Purgatory as it is said, he had a vision of the punishments of Hell while visiting there in 431AD.

The motivation was that as a reward for our pain and suffering, I would pass my exams. Thank God, she was right because having to repeat either the Leaving Cert or Lough Derg would have filled me with dread.

"We'll have to go back in thanksgiving" she said

"Yeah" I replied while thinking *'not a chance!'*

I was by now, singing solo every Sunday morning in the Rock chapel for 11 o'clock Mass. I would never have had the confidence to do that had Sr. Sheila not been right at my side, encouraging me as she played the church organ. I was always very nervous, especially when I had to sing a Psalm, but she gave me such encouragement that I would become oblivious to the crowd of people listening and the fact that the congregation were seated behind us and out of sight was of enormous help.

I loved to sing. It was something I could do freely. As a child it was something I preferred to do on my own because I would have been too shy and self-conscious to sing in front of anyone other than my family. I would trek up over the fields opposite our house and just sit on my own singing or cycle to Rossnowlagh and sing with the monks as they said mass in the Friary.

At home Mum would sing around the house while doing the housework even though she was tone deaf. She usually sang the same couple of lines of a song and always off key.

♫ *"Her eyes, they shone like diamonds,*
you'd swear she was queen of the land.
With her hair flung over her shoulders,
Tied up with a black velvet band." ♫

48

Dad could sing and sometimes at night he would turn off the T.V. and we would all sing together. His special request was that I sing Amazing Grace.

In 1976 the latest and last addition to the family arrived, a baby boy called Padraig. He weighed little more than a bag of sugar and was the cutest wee thing! He was so tiny that Michelle and I could put the shoes of her Crolly doll on him. Cathy even put him in her doll's pram one day so that she could bring him for a walk round the Rock.

That same year Dad got sick and the doctors could not figure out what was the problem. For two years Mum and he were sent to various hospitals for test after test.

Finally, he was diagnosed with lung cancer and due to the long delay, the prognosis was not good. After removing one lung and part of the other, he was told that his condition was terminal. He was not even 40 years old.

We were to find out years later that on the day he learned that he could not be cured he made a deal with God to allow him to be around to see his youngest son make his Confirmation and then he would go without a fight. At the time the doctors told him he could not possibly live beyond 5 years, but the deal was made. He died the year after Padraig made his Confirmation and was buried on Father's Day, 1987.

I sang Amazing Grace at his funeral in the Rock chapel.

I could not come to a decision about entering the religious life. I felt that it was something I really wanted to do and could not understand what was holding me back. Sr.Sheila was very supportive and insisted that I feel no pressure to do anything in haste.

One day while Sr. Sheila and I were walking the beach in Rossnowlagh we met some friends of hers, a married couple called Willie and Brigid from Cavan. They had a holiday home in Rossnowlagh and Sr. Sheila had known them for a long time. They were a lovely couple and invited us both to their home for tea. They spoke about friends of theirs, also from Cavan who needed a childminder.

There was a certain amount of urgency to filling the post as their friends were a professional couple with two young children and a third expected within a few weeks. Afterwards Sr. Sheila suggested that it may be ideal for me at least until I decided what I wanted to do.

Within a couple of weeks, it was arranged that I travel to Cavan with Willie and Brigid to meet the Donagher family.

I was very anxious about the whole thing not least because it was a 'live-in' position and I was uneasy at the thought of living with the family. Being in a house with a man who I did not know terrified me. I only felt safe with the men who were related to me. Other than Dad's friend Alan, my only experience of men outside of my family was abuse. Although I had also been abused by a woman, I felt I was more at risk from men, maybe because I had been abused by so many.

The job was Monday to Friday with most weekends off. On the weekends that I chose not to go home to Donegal, I would stay in the house or go to the convent in Tyrone. Of course, I also doubted whether I was in any way qualified for the job. Baby-sitting for the neighbours' children occasionally did not make me an *au pair* but the fact that Mrs. Donagher would be on maternity leave for a few months reassured me some way. Moving away from home was also very daunting but liberating too as I saw it as being my first step in leaving behind the abuse. Although, I was not being abused at that time, I felt that I could leave all the pain behind me and start again as though the abuse never happened at all.

I promised myself a whole new life as I sat in the back of Willie and Brigid's car going up the Shore Road into Enniskillen towards Cavan.

The Donagher home was just about a mile or so outside Cavan town and when we arrived there were a group of children playing in the front garden and Brigid introduced me to two in particular, a boy aged 7 and a girl 6. I stayed in the garden with the children as Willie and Brigid continued walking around the side of the house to the back door. The boy, Sean was shy but his sister, Yvette was very talkative. They were playing 'Tag' and allowed me to join in. It was quite a while before Brigid called for me to go in and meet Mr. and Mrs. Donagher. I was happy playing with the children and felt very nervous having to go inside to meet my employers.

Bernard Donagher was a mountain of a man and my hand totally vanished as he held it in his.

"Arylene welcome to our home".

He spoke with a strong, proud Cavan accent as he introduced me to his wife Rene. I was surprised at how gentle his voice was and I felt instantly at ease, which for me was very strange.

Rene remained seated while she held her new-born son in her lap. Her smile was her welcome as she introduced me to Finn, who continued to sleep contentedly in the security of his Mother's arms. I was suddenly aware that this family were going to play a significant part in my life and my fears immediately disappeared.

By this time, I had developed a kind of 'radar' and was somehow able to pick up signals when I was in danger from an abuser. I do not know if it was something in their body language or if it was in the way they spoke but somehow, I had learned to recognise when I was in a dangerous situation. I knew there was no such risk in this new environment.

From the instant I arrived I was treated like one of the family and it felt as though I was not there to do a job at all. In fact, I have no recollection of being given any duties or of being told what to do.

When the time came for Rene to return to work, I just continued to do what she and I had been doing together for the last three months and I felt confident enough to do that. If at any time I found myself unable to deal with a situation Rene had put in place a number of back-up plans but the one I relied on most was the comfort of knowing that next door was a lady who had reared a number of children and was affectionately known, by everyone on the street as 'Mam Sully'.

Finn was happy to stay with me and was, by now settled into a routine. That's not to say he always stuck to it! He was a wee character and even at such a young age he had his own personality. I loved him and he knew it. Sean and Yvette were fantastic and were very content to be with me when their parents were out at work. While Finn was asleep, I played football with Sean or 'dress up' with Yvette and we all got on well together. I loved being with the children and felt privileged to be a part of this beautiful family.

My work- day ended when Rene got home but I never clocked on or off and was happy to be around in the evening when the whole family was home. I could come and go as I pleased but I had no interest in going to any of the pubs or clubs in the town and for quite a while I seldom left the house of a night-time.

My favourite pass-time was to read. I loved getting lost in the stories of other peoples' lives. I imagined that I was living those lives which were free from abuse. I pretended it never happened to me and sometimes it worked. But the thoughts and the confusion did not stay suppressed for long. It was naïve of me to think that leaving Donegal would allow me to leave behind the abuse. It came with me, in my head, in my heart, in my being. It consumed me and yet I could never put a name to how I actually felt. I had spent so much time being afraid and on alert there was no room left for being angry or even being hurt. I just survived on a day to day basis and did the best I could to push it all away.

Both Bernard and Rene's jobs were Monday to Friday, so this meant I had weekends off. Initially I spent a lot of weekends at home in Donegal and others in the convent but as I became more settled, I frequently opted to stay in Cavan. This was not surprising as I grew to feel more and more a part of the family and Donaghers, my second home. I felt very safe there and because of that, my confidence was beginning to grow.

It is said there is a lake for every day of the year in the County of Cavan so there was a variety of choice when bringing the children swimming in the summer months. Lough Annagh was a favourite spot to spend a Saturday afternoon. Bernard would happily tog out and join Sean and Yvette for a swim whereas Rene and I were very content to remain fully clothed and paddle with Finn on the fringes of the lake. Rene would have prepared a picnic and an added treat was ice-cream for everyone on the way home.

On a Sunday morning we would all go the Cathedral for mass. I especially loved the 11o'clock mass because the choir generally sang. There were about thirty singers in the ensemble, both men and women. The harmony of the tenor and the bass voices blending with the soprano and the alto, as they prayed in song, always gave me goose bumps.

Willie and Brigid regularly had coffee in the Donagher house after Mass and I would go to my room or play with the children as the friends chatted. One Sunday, however, I waited to have a word with Willie about how I might join the choir. As he was a choir member and someone I knew, I felt more at ease speaking with him rather than having to make inquiries at the Parochial House myself.

Willie offered to bring me to the next choir practice and introduce me to the choirmaster, Father Thomas. On the following Thursday evening, I was excited but also very nervous as I walked with Willie around the back of the Cathedral towards a door that I had never noticed before. I was not the kind of person who would be, in any way, forthcoming and not at all confident when meeting new people so I was growing more and more anxious with every step I took.

"Don't worry", Willie said.

"The audition only lasts about 45 mins!"

Terror struck, and I stopped dead in my tracks, mouth open, unable to speak.

Then I noticed the smile on Willie's face as he continued walking and I realised that he was joking with me.

I really liked Willie. He had a devilish sense of humour and made everything seem like fun. I often wondered if this exasperated Brigid because it was as though he was never serious about anything. She never showed any sign of annoyance though, in fact it was quite the opposite in the way they comfortably showed their love for one another.

We went through the door and entered a room that seemed to be too small for the number of people in it and was made even smaller by a big black piano which sat in the top corner and rows of pews which dominated the rest of the floor space. Everyone huddled into small groups chatting and I felt like an interloper.

Willie introduced me to a few of the older ladies and they immediately welcomed me by saying how nice it was to have younger people in the choir.

Willie then introduced me to Father Thomas who was standing by the piano, busy organising his music sheets in preparation for the start of the practice. My audition entailed being asked if I sang with a choir before, to which I replied sheepishly "Yes Father" and if I knew which section, to which I replied, "soprano Father".

Fr. Thomas then instructed me to stand with the other sopranos as he remained standing to play the piano with one hand and to conduct the choir with the other. Except for Willie I never really got to know any of the other choir members even though I sang with them for almost two years.

During this time, I took night classes and got a diploma in Religious Studies but still, I was very much a loner and never really got to know my classmates either.

Bernard and Rene were involved in the community and were members of various groups and organisations. What I admired most was, neither of them played 'lip-service' while sitting on a committee but rolled their sleeves up to get a job done rather than just talk about it. Bernard was very enthusiastic with the G.A.A. (Gaelic Athletic Association) but he also worked tirelessly helping the less well-off people of Cavan.

He raised funds and ran events as well as working as a volunteer in the homeless shelter a couple of nights a week. I helped when I could, but I was just too shy to ask people for donations and was much better suited to helping out in the shelter.

In fact, I loved being in the shelter as I felt so much more at ease working with people rather than fund raising. Somehow, I felt that I had something in common with the people who stayed there. I was not homeless, but I did not feel part of what might have been thought of as *'normal society'* either. It was presumptuous of me to think that any one of these people thought of themselves in that way, but I felt some kind of affinity none the less.

I never felt like I really belonged anywhere or connected to other people even the people I loved and was close to. I wondered what it might be like to be 'normal' and envied people who did not feel the way I did. I also envied the people who possibly did feel this way but did not have to lie about it. Keeping up the act, pretending to be normal and forever wishing I was, was so exhausting.

One of the regular visitors to the shelter was Old Tom and my introduction to his antics was memorable. He arrived one wet, cold winter's night and appeared to have had one or two too many drinks. He was soaked through and very hungry. He sat down in front of the Calor gas fire while I got him a bowl of hot, thick soup with buttered bread doorsteps on the side.

When I returned with the soup, I could smell something burning and it was coming from the direction of Old Tom. I could see the steam rising from his wet clothes and it was obvious that he was sitting too close to the fire. His trouser leg was singeing but Old Tom was completely oblivious, which I assumed was due to the fact 'he'd had a skinfull'. The heat must have been scorching his leg inside the trousers and I quickly raced over to move his leg out from the fire.

"Feck's sake Tom, you're burning yourself!" I shouted

frantically.

I screamed in terror as his leg came away in my hand!

I was instantly relieved when I realised the leg was artificial and everyone in the room, including Old Tom, were openly laughing at how well the trick had worked yet again. It was the regular stunt pulled on any new volunteer to the shelter. When I got over the shock, I had to admit it was one hell of an initiation and I was pleased to have passed with flying colours. I did not feel in the least bit embarrassed at being caught out.

Actually, I felt honoured to be accepted and felt safe and very comfortable among these people.

The longer I lived with the Donagher family the more difficult it became to contemplate leaving, but I knew I would have to make a decision at some stage about what I would do with my future. My time in Cavan was never deemed to be long-term although it was now almost 3 years since I had moved in. There were two reasons why I had been in no great hurry to leave, firstly I was still massively unsure about entering the religious life and secondly, I really loved this family, especially Finn and the thought of leaving was just too painful.

Since that first day of meeting the children in the garden, I was very aware of how it had impacted on me what it meant to be a child growing up free from abuse and I immediately felt a sense of caring and responsibility for Sean and Yvette, which never wavered. The jolt of admiration I felt as I was introduced to Rene and the feelings of affection for the baby boy in her arms were instantaneous and grew ever deeper over time.

Ironically though, it was Bernard who became the most influential member of the family, as I realised that I never felt the need to be cautious around him, even on the numerous occasions when he and I were alone. This was quite a shock to me because although I knew that not every man that I came into contact with was an abuser, I never thought that I could live in such close proximity with a man and not be afraid. Apart from my family and Alan Carlton, who was as close as family, I would be on constant alert whenever I was in the company of men. My past experiences had taught me to be suspicious and very wary, but Bernard allowed me to experience something that was very different and previously alien to me. From that initial meeting I just knew I was going to be safe which only added to the difficulty of my having to make the decision to leave.

Chapter 3

In the late 70's and early 80's Ireland's economy was in Recession. Young people were leaving in droves, some going to America and some to Britain. My older brother Keith was in Tyrone, my sister Michelle was in New York and my younger brother Gavin was in London. The two youngest Cathy and Padraig were still in school in Donegal. I decided to go to London, on a sabbatical of sorts, to see if a break away would help me to make a decision about my future.

When the day of my departure arrived, I travelled by bus from Donegal to Dublin and got the ferry to Holyhead in Wales. The crossing took over 3 hours and the boat was packed with travellers. The majority of the passengers were young people, speaking with a vast variation of Irish accents, each representing the County they called home. The train journey from Holyhead to London took another 3 hours and finally I arrived at Euston Station.

My brother, Gavin had moved to London the previous year and he had agreed to meet me at the entrance to the 'Underground', the railway system that linked the entire city by high speed trains careering along below ground level. I sought out the big red circle with the blue line through it, the logo that Gavin had described, indicating the place where I needed to be.

As I made my way across the crowded forecourt I hustled and weaved like a footballer in Croke Park on 'All Ireland' final day. I felt unusually confident as I jostled through the throng of people, every one of us on a mission to be somewhere in particular. I arrived at the meeting place to find that Gavin had not arrived yet. I looked around for an out-of-the-way spot to put down my rucksack and sat on it while I waited for him.

The concourse was a hive of activity and it seemed strange to me as I realised that I was so at ease in the mayhem. I was not at all anxious that Gavin was late and almost hoped that he would not appear too quickly as I took in my surroundings. Although there was a wide variety of shops as well as various food and drinks outlets the majority of people were congregated in one area, necks craned as they studied the Information Board, checking the departure and arrival times of the overhead trains. So focused were they on their task, they seemed oblivious to the constant movement of people around them, people all moving quickly, some even running, most looking straight ahead not engaging with anyone, all en-route to a chosen destination.

The diversity of the crowd was not initially obvious to me however after further scrutiny it was very apparent that within this one gathering there was a range of people with various racial, ethnic, socioeconomic and cultural backgrounds as well as different lifestyles, experiences and choices. There were the stereotypical business professionals wearing suits and carrying briefcases, the music lovers of the Punk genre sporting brightly coloured Mohawks, and wearing Dr. Martin boots, the man sitting with his dog, on a dirty blanket holding a hand-written sign saying "Homeless" and non-descript others like me who were simply just getting from one place to another as they sauntered along listening to their 'walk-mans' while reading the headlines in the 'Standard', the London newspaper.

What fascinated me most was how strangely quiet the scene was. Everyone was very purposeful and preoccupied. The only voice audible was the monotone of the public announcer stating which train was about to arrive or depart, to or from which platform. Other sounds blended into a low hum and permeated the huge building. The atmosphere was frenetic and exciting!

I immediately fell in love with the anonymity of this cosmopolitan city and its ability to make me feel invisible, inconsequential and free! I really felt, for the first time, that this was my chance to leave the abuse behind me. I believed that by the time I was due to return home, I would have dealt with all the pain and confusion and would be able to see clearly what I was meant to do with my life.

I was still so immersed in the awe of it all that I did not notice Gavin and his partner Linda coming towards me.

"Yo Sis" he said, apparently for the second time.

"You were away in a world of your own. Are you ok?" he asked anxiously.

"Yes!" I replied excitedly, as I jumped up to hug them both.

Gavin lifted my rucksack and went on to say that he and Linda had taken a couple of days off from work to help me to settle in. Although they had planned to include a very basic tour guide of the most well-known sights such as Buckingham Palace, Big Ben and Trafalgar Square, they advised that there were things I needed to learn about my new environment which were necessary to enable me to get around safely and efficiently. In order to do that I had to become competent in how the Underground system worked.

My first lesson began immediately as Gavin went through the process of purchasing a ticket from a machine and then explained the colourful and intricate map of the London Underground Stations. He confidently strode towards the correct escalator to bring us below ground and quickly found the right platform to allow us to board the train we needed.

The network was popularly known as *the tube* but whether this was in reference to the trains' cylindrical shape or to the miles of underground tunnels they raced through, I do not know.

After we boarded the train it quickly gathered speed and my ears popped. This may have been because of the movement of the train in and out of the tunnels between stations or due to the speed at which it did it. Gavin outlined our journey from Euston to Finsbury Park on the light blue coloured Victoria Line, where we changed to get on the dark blue coloured Piccadilly Line to travel to Bounds Green. Within half an hour we were walking down Brownlow Road to where Gavin and Linda lived.

The house was divided into 4 bed-sits. Gavin and Linda had a large double on the ground floor, the first floor had a smaller double and a single and the top floor had a single bed-sit and the bathroom for the whole house. Gavin had arranged with the landlord for me to have the single one on the top floor. This meant that I had complete privacy and independence while having the security of family at the foot of the stairs.

My bed-sit overlooked the residential road from the front of the house although the one window was so small and positioned in such a way that the view from it was not pertinent. The small room, which I think would have been labelled the box room, contained a single bed, a wardrobe, and one armchair. This meant that if at any time I had a guest, the bed had to be used as a sofa.

The rest of the room was taken up with a kind of

kitchenette which had a sink, a miniature two ring cooker that sat on top of a low fridge, both of which I imagined might have been used in a caravan and a hand-crafted breakfast bar with two shelves.

On one shelf there were 2 dinner plates, 2 side plates and 2 small saucepans. A tall plastic container housed some mixed cutlery.

The other shelf was presumably for keeping food as it was clear of any kitchen ware. An electric kettle, surrounded by 3 mismatched mugs stood on top of the makeshift piece of furniture and if I had the foresight to fill the kettle before going to sleep, I could make myself a cup of tea in the morning without even having to get out of bed. This was my palace and I absolutely loved it!

Gavin and Linda invited me to have dinner with them on my first night and they reassured me about the things I had to do as I adjusted to living in a city. My personal safety was Gavin's main concern and he advised me around some practicalities that I would have to put in place e.g. making sure that I did not miss the last train home or falling asleep on the last train and ending up stranded in Cockfosters, at the end of the line.

I was so excited about this whole new life ahead of me and by the time they were both ready to go to bed I was still wide awake, and I doubted that I would sleep that night. As I climbed up the stairs to my own room, I was determined to put every effort into this experience and looked forward to what the future would bring.

Living on my own and undertaking the responsibilities that go with that was an entirely new concept for me. Although I knew that Gavin was around should I need him, I was eager to take control of my own life and that involved paying my own rent and bills. To do that I needed a job.

Gavin and Linda were both in the hospitality trade, Gavin a chef and Linda a waitress and they said that there was no shortage of jobs available in that field. I had no qualifications or training in that particular area, but I felt that my past experience of working during school holidays in Ann O'Neill's restaurant in Ballyshannon would 'stand me in good stead'.

Indeed Gavin, who also worked in O'Neill's, attributed his own choice of career to Aunty Ann, the endearing title all the younger members of staff gave the proprietor, when he decided to go to Killybegs Catering College in Donegal, after he finished school.

Early the following morning the three of us were on our way to The Shamrock Agency in Greenford, to find me a job.

The Shamrock Agency was an employment centre that helped people find work in all areas of the hospitality business. The summer season had ended but they still had a number of positions available in Hotels, Restaurants and Pubs, all in and around London. Although Ireland's recession caused massive unemployment there was no evidence of it here and I had a number of jobs to choose from. I was less than confident so I thought being a chamber maid was something I could manage. I agreed to attend for an interview the following day in a hotel in South Kensington.

I did not realise how big a journey it was going to be, travelling early through the city from where I lived in Bounds Green. Thankfully though I did not have to worry about switching trains as South Kensington underground station was on the same tube line, the Piccadilly. This meant that I did not have to struggle with how to change lines and gave me the opportunity to get to know the system when out on my own.

Once we had dealt with the priority of my getting a job it was still very early in the day, so Gavin asked me what part of London I would like to visit but it was impossible to decide as there was so much to see.

Travelling from Greenford back into the city, Linda suggested we go to the famous Oxford Street and although I had neither the inclination nor the money to go shopping, I agreed to just follow their lead.

It was decided that getting off the tube at Marble Arch would mean we could then walk the best part of Oxford Street and see all the amazing stores that I had only ever heard of. As we got off the tube and made our way towards ground level, I was amazed at how confident my escorts were in finding the right escalator to bring us to the exit we needed, among the very tight crowd of people.

We stepped out into the moving mass on Oxford Street and immediately headed away from the exit so that we could stop and get our bearings without causing a hold-up. As I took in the atmosphere of the almost tangible buzz in the air, Linda suggested a coffee and a sit down in order to discuss the plan for the day.

We managed to get seats in a coffee bar in the legendary Selfridge's, and as we sipped the scalding, thick espresso Linda excitedly told me about the abundance of wares available on several floors in the famous department store.

"Seriously Arl, it's fantastic for Christmas shopping," she said.

"You can get all your presents in one place".

"Lin, it's not close to Halloween yet and you're talking about Christmas!" I wailed.

"I can't think about Christmas and buying presents

65

when I'm not sure I have a job yet!"

"Don't worry, you'll ace that interview tomorrow", she said reassuringly.

When we finished our drinks, we continued on our journey, meandering around slow-moving pedestrians and keeping pace with those who were able to *window shop* without having to come to a complete standstill. We passed Debenhams, The House of Fraser and John Lewis before heading down into Regent Street and on into Piccadilly Circus.

Piccadilly Circus was exactly how I had seen it on T.V. with its famous illuminated advertising hoardings which were very impressive, even in daylight. The place appeared frantic with traffic coming and going in all directions. Every conceivable mode of transport fought to gain an inch of space around the ring of the circus, which refers to the fact that it was once a complete roundabout or circle until Shaftsbury Avenue was built.

In the centre there is a fountain, on which stands a statue of a winged archer that I and many others mistakenly believed to be Eros, the God of Love. It is in fact, Anteros, the Angel of Charity and was erected in memory of Lord Shaftsbury, a famous Victorian philanthropist.

Cars, vans and motorbikes cajoled with one another to gain ground, but the famous London Black Cab manoeuvred expertly and without hesitation as it ferried passengers around the city with apparent ease. Death defying couriers on bicycles weaved in and out through the traffic carrying envelopes and parcels to various offices and businesses, with the same urgency of the battlefield carrier pigeons delivering messages across enemy lines.

The London Buses were unique. Red, double-deckers

called Route Masters were jammed with people, some obviously in a hurry, but not getting to where they needed to be with any great speed. The passengers on the top deck appeared to be unconcerned as they sat back smoking whereas the passengers on the lower deck, who were not permitted to smoke, constantly looked around as though struggling to decide whether they should remain on the bus or if they might actually get to their destination quicker by walking. Some took their life into their own hands as they jumped off the back of the old R.M. while others jumped on, sometimes with the assistance of the outstretched hand of the 'clippy'.

The 'clippys' otherwise known as conductors, moved up and down between decks, taking fares and spinning out tickets from the machines that hung from around their necks. They shouted to inform the passengers of the stops coming up and were extremely knowledgeable about the tourist attractions and how best to get to them. It appeared as though they wore concrete boots when they swayed with the momentum of the moving bus.

They never stumbled as they walked along the aisles and expertly managed the spiral staircase between decks while at the same time signalling to the driver, who was isolated in the small cab at the front, when a passenger needed to get off at a stop. This was done by tugging on a string that ran along the roof on either side of the bus, from front to back on both decks, which rang a bell. It was ingeniously simple, one tug to *stop* and two tugs to *go*.

Amidst all of this mayhem was the sound of piped music from various shops and other outlets, the wail of emergency vehicle sirens rushing to tend to the needs of the city's residents and visitors which only momentarily silenced the voices of the street sellers and buskers and the continual high pitch beeping of the traffic lights and pedestrian crossings, as well as the perpetual undertone of human communication all of which gives credence to the saying "This place is like Piccadilly Circus!" the phrase a person might use when describing a noisy, chaotic scene. The whole scene was something that I had never experienced before.

It was by now, well into Autumn, but the weather was still quite mild. For my family living on the North-West coast of Ireland it was more than likely to be very different. The biting chill of the sea air blowing in from the Atlantic Ocean and the rain that follows it, ensures that the inhabitants of my hometown in Donegal always have ample opportunity to make full use of their Winter wardrobe.

Those living on the South-East coast of England, however, embrace the warming breeze flowing across from Europe, while Londoners have the added warmth of the heat generated by the city itself. Although I had spent my life enduring the sometimes-harsh weather of my homeland, I was what my Mum would call a *"cauld crather"* (cold creature)and so I welcomed the milder climate of what was to be for now, my new home.

While still under Gavin's confident guidance we walked from Piccadilly Circus to Trafalgar Square where, it seemed, everyone pigeon in London gathered. The bags of seed being sold by vendors was used to entice the birds to flock into this one area and I was much less aware of Nelson's Column and the Square's iconic Stone Lions than I was of the pigeons perched on my hands and on top of my head.

Apart from the obvious giveaway of allowing these creatures to clamour all over a person, there were other tell-tale signs of who were tourists and who were more likely to be people living and working in and around the West End of the city. The sight of a camera dangling from a wrist or slung over a shoulder was a good clue, the intense concentration of someone studying the A-Z book of London's streets was another. But the arm-length twisting and turning of the broadsheet size map of the Underground System was the ultimate indication that this person was a visitor.

Although I had a camera, had been instructed by Gavin to buy an A-Z at the first opportunity and was certainly very unfamiliar with the labyrinth of the Underground I did not *feel* like a tourist...I could easily envision myself as a surrogate Londoner, because I already felt so at ease here.

It was just a short walk into Theatre-Land and Leicester Square but by now I was really tired. Gavin assured me that it was only yards to Chinatown, and it would be well worth the extra walk to taste the most amazing Chinese food served in the restaurants there.

As a chef his enthusiasm about food was understandable but for me it was certainly very different

I had the same ambivalence towards food now that I did with so many other aspects of my life. My only motivation for eating was that it was solely a life support system. I viewed it simply as a biological necessity, the fuel needed for survival. Because of my way of thinking I felt the enjoyment that everyone else associated with eating, was for me, greedy and self-indulgent. Foods considered to be a means of nurturing, self-soothing or a treat, for me were unnecessary and gluttonous.

This was just another issue that made me feel so different to everyone else.

I never associated this with any concern about body-image, it was how I felt about me on the inside – not about how I looked on the outside. I always felt like two people, one 'me' from my view, the other 'me' from other peoples' view and they never matched up. The abuse made me see myself and the world in a different way. I never voiced how I felt because it was very apparent that other people did not think the same way I did, so I participated in the charade of being 'normal'.

Gavin led Linda and I into Gerrard Street and as we walked under the impressive arch of the huge, very oriental gates even I did not need to scrutinise the A-Z to realise that we had arrived in Chinatown.

It seemed as though I had been asleep and just awakened in China! We had instantly stepped into another culture. The entire area was decorated with dragon sculptures, stone lions, lanterns and coloured lights. Almost every doorway was an entrance to an eatery of sorts. Numerous restaurants with cooked ducks hanging from a rail in the front window, authentic supermarkets selling exotic fruit, vegetables and spices as well as bakeries and other outlets offering only Chinese fare. There were some Chinese inspired trinket shops with paw waving cats for sale and one or two clothing shops showing mannequins wearing floral dresses or Kimonos. Even the street sign was bilingual, written both in English and Chinese.

I had no idea how Gavin decided upon a particular restaurant as there were so many to choose from but as Lin and I followed him down a spiral of stone steps into a basement he declared,

"This is a good one!"

Early the next morning I was getting ready to set out on my first solo excursion across London to attend a job interview for chambermaid in one of the big hotels in South

Kensington. Linda came up to my room to wish me luck and said that she and Gavin would meet me that evening in Covent Garden to hear how I had got on. As I made my way to the tube station, I was pleased that I had allowed myself extra travel time in case I ended up on the wrong train and had to double-back. I had managed not to get lost and so arrived at the hotel with half an hour to spare.

This gave me an opportunity to go over in my head the answers I had prepared in reply to the most predictable questions I was likely to be asked during the interview. I was obviously very unaware of the protocol for such an event as I waltzed up the front steps and attempted to enter the plush hotel reception area 15 minutes later. I was abruptly stopped in my tracks by the outstretched arm of a man standing on the top step wearing a long red coat braided with gold thread around the collar and cuffs and donning a red top hat.

"Where are you going young lady?" he asked in a very posh accent.

"I have a job interview", I said.

"Staff round the back", he instructed as he thumbed the direction of the staff entrance behind the hotel.

Any semblance of confidence I had after successfully mastering the tube journey instantly evaporated as I anxiously made my way around the corner.

I found a door marked 'Staff Only' and as I entered was met by a woman in a blue suit who asked my name.

"Arylene Murphy", I answered. "The Shamrock Agency sent me".

She did not volunteer her own name.

"This way", she said.

She led me towards a long row of lockers and stopped at one. She unlocked it then handed me the key.

"£10 key deposit will be taken out of your first pay packet", she informed me.

I could see the locker housed a hoover, a mop and bucket, various spray bottles of cleaning products and furniture polish as well as cloths and sponges. A single coat hanger held a smock with the name of the hotel stitched on the front.

"Your rooms are 201, 202, 203 and 204. Housekeeping staff are not permitted to use the lifts", she stated before she strode off.

I stood dumfounded and thought, 'at least I got through the interview!

Reeling in the wake of the whirlwind left by the woman in the blue suit, 2 girls wearing matching smocks arrived and offered to 'show me the ropes'.

They whisked me off, hauling the entire contents of the locker between us. We went up 4 flights of stairs until we finally stopped outside room 201. There was little time for chit-chat as they immediately began to show me exactly what I was supposed to do. Everything had to be done in a very particular fashion to ensure that each and every room was identical to the other. Beds were made with specific dimensions, towels hung a certain way over rails, and even the toilet roll had to be fitted with the paper draped over the roll and not behind it.

We worked for 4 hours without a break and I hated every minute of it.

The work was hard and poorly paid but what I struggled most with, was the disgusting state of the rooms left by some of the patrons. My fellow workers told me that chambermaids were expected to change soiled sheets and clean filthy bathrooms without question or complaint.

"Only last week there was a stained mattress in a room I was cleaning", one of the girls said. "I rang reception to ask for help to carry it down to the laundry room. I was told that all the porters were busy, and I had to bring it down by myself".

"What?" I shrieked. "What did you do?" I asked.

"I wanted to tell them to *piss off* ", she replied.

"But I really need the job, so I dragged it down 6 flights of stairs on my own!"

I was horrified and knew that I did not want to be a chambermaid for too long.

Finally, my shift was over and although I was really tired, I was looking forward to meeting up with Gavin and Linda for a drink and something to eat. Covent Garden was on the Piccadilly Line and I remembered passing through it on my way to the hotel that morning. When I got on the tube, I kept a sharp lookout for the names of the stations written on the platform walls until we arrived at Covent Garden. As soon as the doors opened, I moved with the swarm of people getting out and going towards the exit.

I found myself being almost carried by the throng of bodies down a long, dimly lit and very narrow tunnel. This section of the Underground Network was obviously part of the original buildings and whether it was due to an awareness of that or the sudden drop in temperature there a felt sense of something strange in the air.

The crowd moved with confidence and I was happy enough to *go with the flow*. Suddenly the mass stopped and without verbal instruction divided into 3 groups. Each group gathered in a collective silence as they stood in front of a cage-like barrier waiting for a lift to descend. Within minutes the cage was drawn back, and people began to file in before the doors had fully opened. We made our way to the back of what I thought resembled a large wooden crate rather than a lift. It took no more than a few seconds for it to be filled to capacity, each of us packed in, nose to shoulder blade. It struck me that when we got into the lift, we did not turn around to face the direction we had entered but stood facing the back wall.

The doors were closed behind us and the lift rattled and shook as it creaked and groaned and slowly inched its way upwards. My fellow passengers seemed unconcerned as it slightly hesitated and resumed its ascent every-so-often on what I thought might be its last journey. Finally, it came to an abrupt halt and the back wall opened to reveal another cage-like barrier which was being drawn back to allow us to exit.

Only then did I realise that the cage-like structures in front of the doors on either side were being manually operated by a passenger waiting to board. It seemed strange that such an old contraption was in everyday use in a modern, busy place like the centre of London.

Indeed, it felt as though I had just travelled from the depths of the city up to ground level in a completely different era.

A huge sense of relief came over me as I walked towards the exit and the strange atmosphere I felt earlier had now vanished. Emerging from the shadows of the old building into the afternoon sunshine was blinding and it took me a second or two to adjust to the brightness. There was no mistaking I was in the right place as I turned the corner into a huge, open-air, cobbled square.

There were different street entertainment acts going on – all at the same time and people sat or stood watching as they decided on which act they liked best and had earned the handful of change being dug out of pockets and bags. There were magicians, jugglers on unicycles, musicians and dancers, people reciting poetry or passages from a Shakespearian play, doing impressions, clowning or mime. Some were contortionists or escapologists while others sang arias as they performed acrobatics but everyone giving their all to the cheering and appreciative crowd.

I caught sight of an arm waving and realised it was Linda. She and Gavin were sitting in the Piazza Café where we had agreed to meet.

As I made my way towards them, I realised how happy I was to see them.

Throughout the day I had felt very low and wondered if coming to London was not a huge mistake. They were keen to know how my first working day had gone but I was hesitant to say that I really did not like it and even dreaded the thought of going back the next morning.

For some reason I thought that if I told them how I felt that I would be letting them down.

"Come on Arl, tell us about it!", Linda said excitedly.

"Um, not much to tell really", I said.

"But I don't know if I'll stick it though", I added with some reluctance.

"Why?" Linda asked concerned.

I started to talk about what the job entailed when Gavin interjected.

"Go for something else".

"Can I do that?" I asked with new hope.

"Of course, you can!" Linda answered incredulously.

"Go back out to the Shamrock and tell them the girls in yon place are being treated like crap so you're gonna jack it in".

I could not believe that it was so simple.

"Won't they be peeved?" I asked. "After all I've only just started".

"Not at all", Linda said reassuringly.

"Ring them tomorrow and say you'll do to the end of the week to get your wages and then you're out of there".

Linda had a big, bubbly personality and she was so self-confident whereas I was awkward and anxious. I was permanently disappointed in myself and ashamed to voice how incapable I felt at having to go back to the agency to tell them that I did not want to continue working in the hotel. Even thinking about it made my heart speed up and my body tingle all over.

I hated myself for being so weak and envied Linda her ability to just speak up about what she believed to be right for her and what was not. What I found to be even more impressive was if she did not instantly know it did not worry her. Linda would 'give it a go' and if it turned out to be less than she'd hoped, she would simply change direction and enthusiastically takes on life's next adventure.

I, on the other hand, over-analysed and second-guessed everything, constantly fearful of making a mistake. True to form, I lay in bed that night, unable to sleep. I thought about the phone call I had to make to the Shamrock Agency and worried about what I would say. In my head I scripted a dialog and predicted what might transpire.

When morning finally came, I was so tired and anxious I was tempted to ring the hotel to report sick. I thought that would not bode well so I dragged myself out of bed and prepared myself to face the day ahead.

I was feeling more and anxious as the day went on until finally, I rang the agency and explained the situation. My sense of relief was almost overwhelming when I discovered that Linda and Gavin had been right.

Indeed, the agency was grateful for my offer of finishing out the week and I was given an appointment to return to their office to discuss some of the other jobs available on their books. I managed to finish the week in the hotel without too much drama maybe because I knew that I was leaving.

I felt that my career as a Chambermaid was over and I hoped that the agency would have something other than hotel work. I was not able to be too choosy as I needed to be earning to pay my rent for the coming week. There was a position for a barmaid with an immediate start available and although I was very unsure about it, the woman at the agency said that it was a small public house called The King's Head, on a quiet back street, run by an older married couple and it would be easy work.

"I've already spoken to the landlord", she said.

"And I've explained that you have no experience with the pub trade here, but he asked for you to go for an interview anyway", she continued.

"He and his wife are Irish, and they want to give you a chance".

With the name and address of the pub and some vague directions, I made my way back to the tube station and tried to figure out how to navigate myself from Greenford in the west all the way over to York Way in north London. I managed to get a grip of the underground map very quickly and armed with the London A-Z, I had little or no difficulty in discovering that my destination was within walking distance of King's Cross Station.

I arrived at the pub with time to spare and taking a deep breath, I walked into the public bar. Inside there were a few older gentlemen drinking beer from glass jugs and they all looked in the direction of the door as I walked in.

The man behind the bar asked, "Can I help you love?"

"Yes", I answered. "Could I speak with Mr. Moran please?"

"You're looking at him!" he stated. "You must be from the agency. Hold on a sec and I'll be round to ye".

I stood where I was, feeling very self-conscious as I became aware of the silence that had suddenly fallen on the place. I felt the eyes of the men behind me on my back and was relived, when Mr. Moran and a woman who I assumed was his wife appeared from a door at the side of the bar. He gestured for me to sit with them at a table in the corner as he instructed a younger man to 'hold the fort' for a while.

"This is me other half, Betty and me own name is Jim", he declared.

"The agency said ye don't have much experience, is that right?"

Before I could answer Betty said, "will ye leave the girl alone a minute, ye didn't even ask her, her name?"

"My name is Arylene Murphy", I said shyly and confessed that I had no experience whatsoever.

"I'm not long over from Donegal and have so far only done chambermaid in a hotel in Kensington. I've served drinks when I was a waitress at home though and I can work hard, if you give me the chance". I knew I was babbling on and felt embarrassed when I finally shut up.

"Donegal, ye say, what part?" asked Jim.

"Ballyshannon", I said. "Ye probably never heard of it". I stopped talking before nerves got the better of me again.

"Course we heard of it!", Jim announced.

"Sure, herself is from a wee place called Kincasslagh, where Daniel O'Donnell comes from or so she tells me", he said as he smiled and nodded his head in his wife's direction.

"And sure, I'm a Roscommon man meself".

"No one ever came from Roscommon only yourself!", Betty declared as she smiled and elbowed Jim in the ribs.

"Well now, sure wouldn't I be the lucky man to have two beautiful Donegal girls around the place, so Arylene when can you start?" Jim asked with a beam of a smile on his face.

I was thrilled.

"Now!" I answered while I shuffled out of my jacket and began looking for somewhere to put my bag.

Betty put out her arms to take my things as Jim said, "Righty oh, come on with me".

I followed him behind the bar and although I felt out of my depth Jim was a very patient teacher. It was obvious that I was indeed inexperienced as I had never even heard of some of the requests from the customers. They too were keen to help me, and it was not long until I beginning to feel at ease.

I was amazed at how good I felt and was delighted when Jim declared, "You're gonna be grand, love. Like a duck to water!"

I could not wait to get home to tell Linda and Gavin about my new job. It was a vast difference from how I felt about working in the hotel. However, I did not consider that there might be any difficulty with taking on the post until Gavin asked, "Will you be doing nights sis?"

The pubs in London opened at 11am and closed at 3 in the afternoon and then reopened at 7 in the evening until 11pm. The morning shifts would be fine but if Jim wanted me to work the night shifts, I could understand why my brother would be concerned. King's Cross was a massive station, with both overhead and underground trains. With St. Pancras beside it, the area was a constant hub of activity and was known to be less than salubrious, especially at night.

"I don't know yet Gav. I have to go back in the morning for 10am but I reckon I'll have to take my turn at nights". I said.

"Feck! King's Cross is dodgy at night Arl. Maybe you should tell the Gov'nor you can't do nights". Gavin said.

"But he might not give me the job if I do that!" I wailed. "I really love it and don't want to jack it in after the first day!"

When I returned to work the following day, I was hesitant to bring up the topic of the night shifts. As it turned out, I did not have to. When Jim rang the 'last orders' bell at 2:50pm he said, "Arylene, would ye mind hanging about after closing to sort out the rota?".

"Yeah, sure". I replied.

By 3:30pm the last customer had gone, and the bar was clean and restocked, ready for opening again that evening. Jim was taking the money drawer out of the till when he said, "Come upstairs for a bit of lunch with Betty and meself and we can plan the shifts for the week".

I followed up behind him and as I went, I could hear Betty singing in the kitchen. When Jim and I walked in she looked quite nostalgic as she sang "The Homes of Donegal" in a duet with Daniel O'Donnell, the L.P. that was playing, at full volume on the stereo in the sitting room.

"Jayzes Betty!" Jim shouted. "Will ye turn down yon eejit and his feckin catawawlin?"

Obviously offended, Betty *"harrumphed"* and stomped off.

Within seconds there was silence. Betty was scowling tight lipped as she returned to the kitchen and she began to vigorously stir the pot of soup simmering on the cooker.

"Sure, don't ye know ye have the voice of an angel love", Jim said as he gently put his arm around her shoulders and bent his head to sniff the contents of the bubbling pot.

"Geroff!" Betty protested but she could not disguise the loving smile in her eyes as she made a petty effort to shrug Jim away.

There was a loaf of what looked like homemade, wheaten bread on the table, along with a plate of ham, a block of cheese and a jar of pickled onions.

"Sit yourself down Arylene", Betty instructed, as she carried over a piping hot bowl of beef and vegetable soup and put it down on the table in front of me.

She preceded to do the same for Jim, although he was already sitting and eagerly awaiting his. Finally, she ladled out her own and sat down at the table with us. No one uttered a word and as I looked at Betty and Jim, I was aware of how close they were as a couple. They joked around and wound one another up but their tender looks, and tactile behaviour left me in no doubt about the loving connection they shared.

"Well, love how are you settling in?" Jim suddenly asked.

"Grand", I replied. "How am I doing?". I inquired anxiously.

"You're a natural!" he replied.

I was delighted!

I loved the work and felt that, with some guidance and experience I could be good at it. I was becoming more confident as I learned how to serve a light & bitter or a pint of lager top but heating a pork pie in the microwave was a bit of a setback albeit a minor one. The old fellas, who were everyday regulars in the public bar found it hilarious when I brought out a plate of soggy pastry with meat floating in melted jelly and put it down in front of a guy in a suit for his lunch.

I was mortified when Jim explained that pork pies were made to be eaten cold unlike sausage rolls or Cornish pasties which could be eaten hot or cold.

"Sorry about the pork pie fiasco earlier", I said.

"No worries at all love", Jim said through a smile. "It's a very common mistake. So, let's sort this rota, what shifts can ye do?"

"I can work any day", I answered. "But I'm not sure about the nights".

Jim looked at Betty and said, "Ah, we were looking for full-time bar-staff, weren't we love?"

My heart fell, and the disappointment must have shown on my face because Betty leaned over to pat me on the hand and said,

"Don't worry, we'll work something out".

It was decided that I work 5 morning shifts during the week and 2 nights at the weekend. When I was working the night shift Jim would pay for a taxi for me to get to Kings Cross Station so that I could catch the last tube home to Bounds Green. Within a couple of weeks, we all agreed that this arrangement was working well.

As the Christmas season neared, the pub grew quieter. Apparently, this was not unusual as people prepared for the impending expenses of the upcoming celebrations. This gave me the opportunity to learn more about the functioning of a London pub and it was not long before my confidence began to grow. The daily clientele was predominately local, either living in the tower blocks off York Way or in the houses on ground level, all around the old gas works and the various back streets. Some had lived in the area their whole lives and were very proud of their heritage, though many had constant complaints about how the area had changed and not for the better. The introduction of heroin and its obvious effects further tarnished the pre-existing notorious reputation of King's Cross and its vicinity.

The few 'old timers' who populated the public bar every morning, sat in the same seats and drank pints of real ale from personalised Toby jugs, spoke about the devastating impact this new drug was having on their community.

Although I was very aware of the heroin epidemic in Ireland, as the catastrophic impact of it among young people in Dublin was constantly being reported through the media, the use of any illicit drug was far outside of my own reality.

I knew that some of my old school friends had smoked cannabis on occasion, but I never had the opportunity to try it. I really did not feel that I had missed out on some vital milestone, rather the fear of being out of control in some way, would have undoubtedly discouraged me, had I found myself in a situation where drugs were available. I had spent many years keeping secrets and was constantly afraid of not being strong enough to continue to carry the burden of silence, so the very thought of being, in any way vulnerable around other people terrified me.

I felt as though I was in a permanent state of anxiety, always on alert, fearful of letting the guard slip. Every thought or feeling I shared with another person seemed *fake*. Everything I said, everything I did was an act because if spoke about what I was really feeling my world, such as it was, would crumble.

I was very lonely. Even being around the people who cared about me did not alleviate this sense of 'aloneness'. My only real companion was the voice in my head, forever chattering, analysing, over-thinking and second guessing, constantly trying to figure out what was safe and what was not. It was never my intention to deliberately deceive anyone … I just did not know any other way to cope. I always doubted my perception of things, never trusting or believing in myself to be right about anything and went along with things just to blend in.

This became my way of being. It worked very well in the pub trade because I got on well with everyone. I listened to the woes of the customers and never disputed their opinions. It also worked well for me because I did not have to struggle with trying to figure out what to say or who to be.

It seemed that no length of time had passed when Christmas arrived. Gavin and Linda were going home to Ireland for the holidays, but I chose to stay and go home during the summer instead. The pubs in London open on Christmas Day and I was quite happy to work.

Betty and Jim invited me to have dinner with them and stay the night rather than return to an empty bedsit on my own. Jim decided not to open again until Boxing Night and within an hour of the doors opening the pub was packed with customers. Everyone was still full of Christmas spirit and the atmosphere was jovial. At about 10 o'clock Jim said I could finish early.

"Go you on home love, Betty and I can manage".

"Are you sure?" I asked, as I looked over at Betty who was expertly pouring 3 pints of Guinness, allowing each one to settle before topping it up and handing it over to an eagerly awaiting customer.

"Aye, away you go Arylene. We'll see you in the morning", Betty calmly replied.

I needed no further persuasion as I went out to the

hallway to get my coat and to phone the cab company to bring me from the pub to Kings Cross Station.

Less than 20 minutes later I was standing on the tube platform, waiting for the Piccadilly train and contemplating on how very lucky I was to be working for such kind people. Jim and Betty's approach to their staff was a far cry away from how the management of the hotel in Kensington treated their employees. My time in London could have been very short had I felt obliged to continue working as a chambermaid.

Suddenly a rush of wind came up through the tunnel and the train tracks began to rumble, signifying the imminent arrival of the tube train into the station. Everyone moved forward, in anticipation of getting a seat, should there be any vacant. They stood with toes on the yellow safety line, like sprinters on their marks in a race as the tube roared along the platform at speed.

When it began to slow down the awaiting passengers jostled along the yellow line trying to judge when and where it might stop. If they judged correctly, they would be standing directly in front of the carriage doors when they opened, giving them pole position in the scramble for an empty seat. As people alighted and boarded the carriages a voice on the sound system repeated "Mind the Gap!" warning passengers of the space between the tube and the platform.

Within seconds the doors closed, and the tube gathered up speed and raced into the black tunnel towards its next stop.

The London Underground is a very quick and convenient way to get around once you become familiar with how it operates. I was both fascinated and thrilled with the almost complete absence of any human interaction among the mass of travellers who used it daily. People sat by side and frequently had to stand in very close proximity and yet never uttered a word to one another. Most were engrossed in some kind of reading material while others listened to music on their Walkman through earphones and all avoiding any real encounter with one another.

My previous experience of frequent travel was when I lived in Cavan and bused home to Donegal. Although I looked forward to getting home, I dreaded the prospect of sitting beside someone who insisted on having an in-depth conversation for the entire journey. Because I was uncomfortable making small talk with complete strangers, in a situation where there was no escape, I always carried a book which I dived into with gusto and enthusiasm the minute I sat down, in order to put up a barrier between myself and my fellow travellers.

In London, I carried a book with the purpose of reading it because there was less need of it as a safety mechanism or prop. However, it was important not to get too enthralled in the story for fear of missing my stop. Each time I felt the tube slowing down I looked up to check what station it was in until it was time for me to get off. My journey took me through Caledonian Road, Holloway Road, Arsenal, Manor House, Turnpike Lane, Wood Green and finally home to Bounds Green.

The next day, I made the same journey back, to begin my morning shift in the pub. When I arrived, it was obvious from the amount of commotion going on in the street that there was something very wrong. The road outside the pub was cordoned off with police cars. An ambulance was up on the kerb directly in front of the public bar and a number of unmarked vehicles were parked haphazardly across both sides of the road. I ran towards the side door to gain access but was instantly stopped by a police officer on guard.

"What's happened?" I screeched.

"Can I have your name please?" he asked.

"Are Jim and Betty ok? What's going on?"

I tried to walk past him to get to the door, but he put his arm out to prevent me from touching the handle.

"This is a crime scene", he said very directly "That has not been dusted for prints yet!"

"I work here", I told him. "Please tell me that Jim and Betty are ok?".

Chapter 4

I had to attend Islington Station the following day to make a statement to the police. They were investigating the circumstances of Jim's death and believed that he may have been attacked when he was closing up that night. Betty found his body in the gents' toilet of the pub in the early hours the following morning. After giving my statement, I walked out of the police station and wandered aimlessly around the streets with little or no awareness of the direction I was heading in.

I thought about Jim as I walked and found it difficult to accept that someone could have murdered him. I thought about Betty and wondered what she might do now. She would undoubtedly be heartbroken. The policewoman who interviewed me said some family members were over from Ireland, so I figured Betty would be with them.

I was at a loss as to what to do now. I stopped to get my bearings and realised I was on the Caledonian Road. I decided to buy a newspaper and then went into the nearest pub for a drink and a sit down. It was lunchtime and the pub was busy but I managed to find an empty table. When I got my drink, I sat down and only then noticed how weary I was. My mind was racing with thoughts of Jim and Betty when suddenly a voice broke in.

"Penny for them". I looked up and recognised Mac, one of the 'old timers' from the King's Head.

"Sorry, stupid thing to say", he muttered, almost to himself.

"Can I get you a drink?" he asked.

"No thanks Mac just got one".

My refusal meant that I did not want company either,

but Mac did not pick up on that.

He put his pint down on the table and sat on the seat opposite me, saying "poor Jim eh?" Before I could comment he carried on, "do they know what happened yet?"

I shook my head in reply and noticed he did not have a personal drinking jug here.

"I suppose the pub will stay closed 'til they figure it out", he stated.

I suddenly realised that I would probably have to get another job. I felt guilty for thinking so selfishly.

It was as though Mac was reading my mind when I heard him say, "You'll be needing a job? They're looking for staff here you know. Why don't you ask?"

Before I could respond to any one of his questions he shouted, "Hey Gerry!" as he stood up to attract the attention of a man collecting the empty glasses from the surrounding tables. The man strode over to us with a row of dirty pint glasses running up the full length of his left arm and a banana bunch of five more held in his right hand.

"Aw right Mac?" he asked.

Before I knew what was happening, I was being interviewed for a job. Gerry was the Manager of the pub and he offered me a trial for that afternoon.

Although the pubs had to close in the afternoons, some operated what was known as a 'Monday Club'. This meant that the doors were locked between 3pm and 7pm but the customers stayed inside, and the bar remained open for service. Because this was a breach of the licencing law the curtains were closed, and the juke box turned off giving the impression the pub was empty to anyone outside, especially if it happened to be a passing police car.

Gerry told me where to put my coat and he started to

show me where everything was behind the counter. The serving area was massive and there were at least double the number of beer taps than in the King's Head. There were rows of optics and I had no idea what might be in some of the bottles. There were cold shelves under the optics packed with all kinds of bottled beers and lagers as well as mixers, juices and other soft drinks. Even the choice of bar snacks was extensive. There were crisps in every conceivable flavour from cheese and onion to beef wellington and Worchester sauce. There was a variety of nuts, salted, plain or dry roasted as well as bacon fries, scampi fries and pork scratchings.

He then gave a quick lesson in how to operate the till and said to 'get stuck in'.

I was very nervous and self-conscious at first, but the customers were fantastic as they instructed me in how to serve each of their preferred drinks. Just as I was beginning to settle into my new post a shout went up from the far end of the bar and it was very obviously directed at me.

"Hey, Murphy serve your *townie* first!"

I quickly spun around but initially did not see anyone I recognised. A *Townie* referred to a person who originated from the same town as yourself back in Ireland and although I continued to scrutinise the crowd, I could not see anyone I knew from Ballyshannon.

In all the time that I had been in London, I had not seen anyone I knew from home and given that it was my intention to leave *'it'* all behind, I thought this suited me very well. But it did not take me very long to realise *that the 'it'* I was referring to, was the abuse and not the people I cared about.

As well as that, with the droves of Irish people moving to England for work it was unlikely that I would never meet a *Townie*, especially as I was working in the pub trade.

"Over here!" the voice shouted again and suddenly I saw a familiar face.

"Johnny the Duck!" I yelled back.

This was a *Townie* that I was very happy to see.

Johnny was the brother of a very special friend of mine that I had to say goodbye to when I decided to move to London. I have no idea how Johnny came to be known as the Duck but his sister, my dear friend Sheila, did not share the title. I was dying to know how Sheila was doing but when I enquired Johnny replied in a typically brotherly fashion saying that she was 'grand.'

Only a few days later Leo Sayer, the pop star whose picture I had on my bedroom wall as a teenager, came into the pub. I was starstruck at having the opportunity to serve him a drink but even that did not outweigh my delight of seeing Johnny the Duck, my best friend's brother from home.

Before too long I was becoming familiar with some of the beers and ales that were previously completely unknown to me. Gerry explained that the Tarmon was a *free house* which meant that they were not tied to a particular brewery, therefore they could sell all kinds of brands of lagers and ales and a variety of spirits and wines.

Gerry was obviously very popular with the customers and his hearty laugh could be heard from one end of the big horseshoe bar to the other.

Although the pub was officially closed the place was packed with afternoon drinkers and we were both kept busy serving customers as well as keeping the bar clean and stocked.

There was a door marked 'PRIVATE' at the side of the saloon bar and just before 7pm that evening a tall, dark haired man came through it. He strode in behind the counter and opened the till to take out all the big notes that Gerry and I had put in throughout the afternoon.

"Who's this?" he asked.

He was talking to Gerry and raised his thumb in my direction.

"New barmaid", Gerry replied.

I stood stock still as I realised that I seemed to have gotten the job.

"Welcome to The Tarmon" he said.

He then strode off again, through the door marked private, taking a bundle of cash with him.

"That's Terry, the Gov'nor", Gerry said.

That day was to be the beginning of a new chapter in my life.

The Tarmon was situated about halfway between Kings' Cross and Finsbury Park Stations on the Calidonian Road, more commonly known as the Cally by the locals. The pub was thought of as an Irish house as most of the patrons were Irish as was the Gov,nor and his wife. Terry and Mary lived on the premises with their 2 young boys as did the full-time staff which included Gerry, a barman named Joe and a chef called Albert. There were 3 or 4 part-time bar staff and Stevie the pot-man who, like me all lived out.

At first, my working week was Monday to Friday, 10am to 3pm. I also worked the Monday Club every week with Gerry which gave me an opportunity to learn the finer details of running a busy bar. Gerry also taught me how to change a beer keg and organise the cellar. During quieter periods I chatted to the regulars and although most were Irish, some were Londoners and others who had come from a variety of places all over the world.

It was never too difficult to remember 'who was who', as

it was common practice to refer to someone by what they drank, the job they did or where they came from. There was pint of Guinness Pat, Mick the mechanic and Kiwi Ken. Londoners also cut names short, even shorter than the shortened version and for some reason, sometimes put an 'L' on the end. The gov'nor Terry, short for Terrance was called Tel and Gerry, which was short for Gerard was always called Gel. I felt very privileged to be given the title Arl, although this was a name I was very accustomed to as it had always been my family's shortened version of my name.

I loved working with Gerry because not only was he teaching me so much about the pub trade, he was always good fun to work with. He never seemed to be in bad humour even when he was nursing a hangover, following his day and a half off. He was originally from Co. Cavan and moved to London to work when he completed his training with Guinness Brewery in Dublin some years beforehand. He was very quick witted and sometimes it was difficult to know if he was joking or telling the truth.

It did not take me long to figure out his sense of humour and even on the busiest shifts he and I had a laugh while still getting the job done. In fact, we really worked well together, and the customers soon started joking about him and I being a tag team behind the bar.

The Tarmon was within walking distance from Pentonville Prison and it was not unusual for the pub to host a party for a group celebrating the release of a friend or family member who had completed their sentence in the notorious detention facility. When I learned that the next Monday Club was to host such a party, I was a little unnerved. I was feeling anxious when the day arrived, and Gerry was trying to be reassuring as he explained that the young man being released was a local lad and the son of one of the regulars.

"His name is Mark, Jameson Pat's young fella", Gerry said.

"There'll be no trouble". (Jameson's was the name of the whiskey that was Pat's usual, hence the nickname)

"What'd this Mark do?" I thought that a reasonable question.

"Don't worry about that" Gerry replied which did not lessen my worries in any manner whatsoever.

"As long as he's not a murderer!" I exclaimed.

Gerry laughed and said, "Na! Bit of a row in a pub, that's all".

I was to later discover that Mark was in a pub brawl which resulted in the landlord being seriously injured. Gerry was obviously trying to protect me from the similarity of this situation with what we had originally thought happened to Jim.

As we were later to learn, the investigation into Jim's death showed that he was not assaulted but that he had had a heart attack and sustained the facial injuries when he fell on the tiled floor in the Gent's toilet. I was certain that this would have been of great comfort to Betty but whether it would mean that she might return to the King's Head, I seriously doubted it. I was not keen to return to work there either and selfishly hoped that Betty felt the same. If she did plan on returning, I would feel obliged to give up my job in the Tarmon and go back with her, simply out of loyalty to both her and Jim.

That Monday club party went without a hitch, in fact it was all very low key. 20 minutes after Mark's arrival I had put the reason for the celebration out of my mind and got on with serving the drinks and snacks. Before I knew it, it was 7

94

o'clock and time to officially open the bar. Although I was tired after 4 hours of helping to keep the party group *'fed & watered'* I felt exhilarated in the atmosphere of a busy pub environment.

That night the Gov'ner Terry asked all the staff to stay after closing to have a drink with himself and the landlady, Mary. I told Gerry that I could not stay because this would mean that I would miss the last tube from King's Cross home to Bounds Green.

"Sure stay over" he said.

With that he strode over to where Mary was sitting, said something to her and came back.

"That's it sorted. You can kip in the spare room upstairs" he stated with a look of satisfaction on his face.

As I began to protest, he said with mock authority, "You're staying and that's an end to it!".

I raised my hand in a salute and replied, "Yes Sir!"

I took a break to have a sit down and something to eat and then went back to help with the night shift.

It was a quiet night so by the time the last customer had left most of the clearing up was done. Terry took the drawer out of the cash register and left it upstairs. When he returned a short time later, he asked everyone what they wanted to drink. I was cautious about my drinking as my limited but detrimental previous experience had led me to believe that alcohol *did not really agree with me.*

My introduction to alcohol was, in hindsight, very telling. Unfortunately, it was a lesson that with time, dimmed in my working memory. Before my 18th birthday I had no interest in drinking mainly because I had intended to enter the religious life. I had tasted a variety of different alcoholic drinks, but I had never been drunk so, to celebrate my birthday, myself and my friend, Marcus decided that it was something that I should do before giving up any opportunity to have this experience.

The plan was that we would go to the Astoria dancehall in Bundoran the following Saturday night and I would get drunk while he stayed sober in order to look after me. This best laid plan went array when both of us got so drunk that I had to be put into a Taxi by 2 other friends who happened to be there. They then carried me to my front door at 3:30am, where I threw up the entire contents of my stomach on the doorstep. I had no memory of any of the nights events however the sickness I endured for the following 3-4 days was something unforgettable for quite some time. This experience of drinking to *blackout* was something that I was to learn many years later, as an indication of my predisposition to alcoholism.

It was some time before I drank spirits again and so more often than not, I drank lager or beer. Gerry quickly informed me that the house rule for *'afters'* was that no beer would be served so I ordered a dark rum and coke. I had never tasted this drink, but I had served it to a customer earlier and thought it smelled nice. As it turned out it smelled better than it tasted but once I had finished the first one the second one was much easier to drink.

The alcohol gave me confidence and I began to tell Gerry about my worries of having to leave the Tarmon, to go back to Betty at the King's Head but he could not understand my thinking at all.

"Don't be silly! You don't owe that woman anything!"

"I feel I do!" I said.

"Herself and Jim were so good to me and I'd feel terrible if I just left Betty on her own".

"That's not your responsibility!" he said incredulously.

This sense of needing to look after other people was something I had always struggled with. When something went wrong for someone I cared about, I always felt that it was, in some way, my fault and therefore it was my responsibility to fix it. I never understood where my boundaries and other peoples, started and ended. If they felt bad, I did too so in order for me to feel good I had to make them feel good.

"But she'll think I'm an awful bitch!" I was almost in tears by now.

"For God's sake! Will you listen to yourself?! Come here to me" Gerry said as he put his arm around me.

I was instantly on alert.

Gerry sensed my discomfort and immediately apologised as he lifted his arm away. I felt foolish for my reaction and responded by apologising to him.

Mary, the landlady was watching the exchange and said "for the love of God! When you two lovebirds stop apologising to one another, one of you get behind the bar and get us all another drink!"

I immediately jumped up and went behind the bar to get myself away from the situation. Everyone started joking about what Mary had said and I felt so embarrassed I was blushing. Of course, this was simply fodder for more joking.

Eventually Terry said, "will you lot leave the girl alone or we'll end up having to look for another barmaid if she packs the job in!"

That was my last memory of the night. Apparently, we all sat drinking into the early hours, but I had absolutely no recollection of anything that I or anyone else had said or done.

The following morning Gerry and I were on shift for

opening the bar and we were both feeling the painful effects of the night before.

"I've had 2 mugs of coffee and 4 Panadol and I still feel awful", I moaned to Gerry when I arrived behind the bar to start on the bottling up.

But I was also feeling something else…FEAR!

"Not feeling the *Mae West* myself", came his response.

"Welcome to life in the Tarmon", he laughed.

The late-night drinking was a regular occurrence he said.

"Did I make a show?" I asked him cautiously.

"Yeah! You were good craic now!" he replied.

My heart started beating faster inside my chest.

"Why! What happened?"

The fear was mounting, and I could feel myself beginning to panic.

"Did I make a fool of myself? Was I talking crap?"

"Aye you gave away all your secrets" he answered in a hushed whisper.

I could feel the blood drain from my head. I felt faint.

He must have seen the terror in my face because he quickly tried to reassure me by saying,

"It's ok. You didn't do anything out of order".

I was not appeased.

"What <u>DID</u> I do?" I asked

"You didn't do anything", he insisted.

I knew that my reaction was just bringing on more attention, so I tried to pass it off a bit.

"From now on I'm sticking to lager," I vowed.

"No way am I drinking like that again", I added.

"Go back upstairs", he said

"Have one of Mary's fry-ups and you'll be grand".

The very thought of eating was making me queezy but when I got as far as the kitchen Mary had a plate of bacon and eggs ready for me.

"Sit yourself down love", she said as I reluctantly sat down at the table.

"You'll feel better when you eat that".

However, even Mary's mothering encouragement was not enough to prevent my stomach's repulsion at the possibility of consuming food. Eventually she gave in and tutted to herself as she removed the plate from in front of me. I felt so guilty and was suddenly afraid that I had made her angry.

"I'm really sorry Mary", I wailed like a child terrified of upsetting its mother, rather than a grown woman who was just too hungover to eat.

I was almost in tears and felt foolish for getting upset.

"Hey darlin, don't worry about it", Mary said.

I have no idea how I managed to get through that day but as I lay in bed later that night, I adamantly vowed that I would never ever drink that much again.

The rest of the week went without a hitch. I loved working in the Tarmon and I seemed to get on well with everyone there. I had all but forgotten my sense of duty to Betty until one evening Terry asked me into the upstairs sitting room for a chat. I was instantly in a panic, assuming that he was, for some reason that I could not fathom, upset with me.

"What have I done?" I asked, frightened.

"You've done nothing", he said reassuringly.

"What's wrong then?" I asked, still afraid.

"Nothing!" he said.

I could see that he was becoming frustrated, so I shut

up, but I was very anxious about what he was going to say, even though I had no idea whatsoever what that was going to be.

"I was chatting to a brewery rep. today", Terry started.

"He told me that Betty will not be going back to the King's Head, in fact she will not be coming back to London at all. She has decided to retire from the pub trade and is going to stay at home with her family in Donegal".

I did not know what to say as so many different emotions were coursing through me, all at the same time, so initially I said nothing.

"You ok?" Terry asked.

"I'm fine, thanks Terry", I replied.

"Take your break now and have a cup of tea. Come back down to the bar when you're ready", he said.

"Thanks Terry", I said again.

I thought about Betty and how heartbroken she must be. She loved the pub trade, but I guess it would be too difficult for her without Jim. I felt ashamed that I was relieved that she had decided not to come back. Her decision removed my turmoil over my sense of duty to her. I felt selfish and disloyal especially as I knew that she would be chuffed for me to have found a place where I was happy. I even knew that she would 'give out' if she was aware of how I felt. I thought about her singing Daniel O'Donnell's *Homes of Donegal* and continued to feel guilty as I washed up my cup and went back down to the bar to resume my shift.

I loved working in the Tarmon and it seemed as though I certainly did have a flair for the job. Over the next few months I got to know all the regulars and what their favourite tipple was. During quiet times I learned more about their families and their lives, but these conversations just reinforced my realisation that I was different. On the surface I was just like many other young Irish girls living and working in London, but I knew that I did not think or feel like other people. I listened and agreed with what was being said but there was always another conversation going on inside my head which totally disagreed with what others deemed the norm. Because of this I worried constantly about my mental health and was always terrified of having a nervous breakdown.

Somehow, Gerry made me feel safe. He was of course unaware of this, but he knew that I always preferred to work with him and so he arranged the staff rota to ensure we were on the same shifts. I was still working the morning shifts, but I was now doing a few more evening shifts as well. My hours now were 10am -3pm and 7pm -10pm. I never worked the late week-end nights because the last tube on the Piccadilly line leaving King's Cross was before midnight.

There was always one night a week dedicated to 'staff afters' and I never missed these late-night sessions. I had become much more comfortable drinking with my work mates and staying in the spare room of the pub had become a regular occurrence.

I discovered that the benefits of drinking outweighed my fears of being drunk.

Alcohol gave me relief from the voices in my head and I felt that I could be a part of normal living, just like everyone else. I always drank to black-out, but I became less fearful of what I might divulge.

It seemed as though the years of keeping secrets had taught me how to behave even when I was not fully in control. I was thrilled with this new- found discovery because it meant that I could get relief from the incessant noise going around in my head.

Summer was approaching and the evenings were brighter for longer and so rather than getting a taxi down to the station when I finished work at 10pm, I would walk. It took about 20 minutes, down the Cally turning right into Brewery Road, and out on to York Way. Left down York Way would take me straight into the back of King's Cross Station. I loved the hub of King's Cross and rather than make my way round to the front of the station I would venture through the back where the reality of life was lodging.

People who were hidden away and out of sight during daylight emerged when darkness fell. Women and men, young and old took up position some at unmarked pitches on Euston Road and others at designated lampposts from the back of the station, up along York Way where they all waited for their customers.

I never felt out of place here because I did not see addicts and prostitutes – I saw wounded people, just like me! I saw the fear and loneliness of isolation, while at the same time the comfort of togetherness and belonging. A part of me connected with these people and I felt more on the 'inside' rather than on the 'outside' as I had always been. I had spent my life peering longingly through an opaque barrier that had separated my world from everyone else's, marginalised and alone.

Initially, I never said anything to anyone, nor them to me. There seemed to be an unspoken agreement around this shared space. I did not feel as though I was intruding, and it seemed that no one else did either. There was no threat, no fear. I cannot pinpoint when this silence was broken but it was not long until some of us were addressing each other by a nod of the head or a quick 'hello'. Somehow, I just knew that no one would welcome any further communication as my hanging around would not be good for business, but I longed for more interaction. This longing was totally pointless because I knew that had I had the opportunity to really talk to someone about how I felt I would have no idea about where to start.

When I arrived home one night, after a busy evening in the pub, I found that Gavin and Linda were waiting up for me. They both worked early mornings in the city, so being up late was very unusual for them. My instant reaction was to believe that something was wrong.

"Everything is ok" Gavin immediately said, obviously reading the worried expression on my face.

"Linda and I have something to tell you".

I followed them into their bedsit and sat down as Linda put the kettle on.

"Tea, Arl?" she asked.

"Yeah please" I said.

"So, come on then. Tell me what's going on"

"Will you wait 'til we get the tea? Then Linda and I can tell you together" Gavin responded.

I sat for what seemed like a very long time until at last the tea was made, and we were sitting, cup in hand each waiting for the other to speak.

Finally, Gavin broke the silence. "Lin and I are going home".

I knew he did not mean that they were going home for a holiday.

"To stay?" I asked.

Linda answered. "Gav got a fantastic job in a hotel in Dublin".

"When are you going?" I asked.

This time Gavin answered.

"We haven't got a definite date yet or handed in our notice here because we wanted to see what you were doing. Are you coming home with us or do you want to stay here on your own?"

"I don't know" I replied. "Its just a bit sudden"

"You'll be fine here on your own if you want to stay", Gavin said.

"Or you can come with us and look for a job in Dublin".

"Let me think about it" I said.

As I lay in bed that night, I thought about what I would do. This was not just a decision about living in London or Dublin, it felt like I was having to decide my future and I did not think I was ready for that. As usual, my thoughts came back to the abuse. It defined everything about me...who I was, how I felt, what I believed and how I behaved. I often thought about who I might be if I had not been sexually abused and yearned for the life that I was *supposed* to be living. The monsters from my childhood took, not only my past but my present and my future.

I thought about returning to Ireland to enter the convent, but I had doubts about my future as a nun, for some time now. For years I truly believed in my calling to dedicate my life to God as a Mercy sister, but I began to question what I previously believed was a vocation. When I thought about why I wanted to enter I knew that a part of me believed the convent was going to be a safe place for me to hide from the world. This, I knew was not the foundation of a true calling. I made the decision to stay in London for the time being.

As Spring moved into Summer the Tarmon got busier and my confidence behind the bar grew. For now, at least, I felt that I had made the right decision in staying on. One evening as I was getting on with bottling up, Gerry asked what I was doing for my birthday which was coming up in a week or so.

"No plans as yet", I replied.

"Why do you want me to work?"

"Naw. I was just wondering" he said.

Confused I carried on with the bottling up.

"Fancy a drink?" he asked

"What, now?" I answered

"Nooo!" His stretching out of the word 'no' suddenly made me realise that he was actually asking me out.

"On a date, you mean?" I enquired

"If you like", he said.

"For your birthday. We could go up the Galtymore."

I was stunned because although we got on so well together, I never thought that he would be interested in me in that way. Gerry was older than me and as the manager I thought of him as my boss.

"No strings" he said as he held his hands up in mock surrender.

"Ok" I said, "Why not?"

I had not dated anyone for a long time and for the life of me, I could not figure out why I had agreed to go.

When I was a teenager, I had a couple of boyfriends but for me this was just another part of 'fitting in' and doing the things my friends were doing. All of my friends had boyfriends and we went as a group to the Astoria dancehall in Bundoran. We came home with self-inflicted whiplash after headbanging all night to the band 'Horslips'. I loved the 'idea' of having a boyfriend then but the fear of having to eventually go beyond kissing and cuddling terrified me.

As I got older, I had no interest whatsoever in dating. The very idea of being intimate with someone frightened me beyond reasoning. I had spent my adult years living in the safety of isolation and would usually be very hesitant to leave that safe place.

For some reason though, I knew that I would be safe with Gerry.

The next Tuesday was my birthday and our date night. I was very anxious as I tried to figure out what I would wear. The Galtymore was a popular Irish club in Cricklewood, North London and when Big Tom & the Mainliners were playing it drew a huge crowd. I knew that I did not own anything suitable for clubbing so, that afternoon I ventured into the shopping mall in Wood Green to buy an outfit. I was content with my purchases but was becoming more and more anxious as the time of Gerry's arrival to pick me up drew near.

I had 6 tins of lager chilling in the fridge so that I could offer Gerry a drink before going out. I decided to have one, in the hope that it would calm my nerves. The first one did not have any great affect, so I had another. I was on my third drink when Gerry arrived, and I was certainly feeling less anxious.

"Starting ahead of me, are you?" Gerry asked

"I only had one", I lied.

I had planned on being careful about how much I would drink on our night out but once I had started drinking, I just drank more. I was beginning to see a pattern around my drinking and noticed that if I did not start to drink, I was fine. But once I took the first drink, I could not stop. The time of being able to enjoy a pint or two seemed far away, even though it was less than a year ago.

I woke up the next morning in a room in the Tarmon.

My last memory of the night before was getting into a taxi with Gerry to go to Cricklewood. I had no recollection of being in the Galtymore or of arriving at the Tarmon and going to bed in the spare room. I felt sick, not just hungover but mortified and terrified about what I might have said or done. I noticed that I was still wearing the clothes I went out in, minus my shoes. I looked around the room but could not find them, so I sheepishly strolled into the kitchen to find Mary, the landlady cooking lunch for the bar.

"Rise and shine finally", she said.

"Hiya Mary", I was too afraid to say anything more.

"Sit down and I'll get you a cup of tea. Then you can tell me what happened" she stated.

That was just the point, I had no idea what had happened, but I could not tell her that. I felt so ashamed and embarrassed and could feel myself going into a panic. I was about to get up from the table and run to the bathroom when Gerry walked in.

"You look as bad as I feel", he said with a big grin on his face.

"For feck's sake Gerry, you can't say that to the girl!" Mary shouted from the top of the kitchen.

I did not know whether to laugh or to cry.

Gerry took me by the hand and said, "Go back to bed for a while. I'll bring you in the tea".

I did as he said and waited anxiously to hear what he had to say.

When he arrived with the tea he sat on the edge of the bed and asked, "how's the head?"

"Gerry I'm so sorry", I said very quietly. "I ruined everything. I'm mortified!"

"Jeez will you calm down?!" he said, "It wasn't that

bad"

Again, I was afraid to say anything more.

"Do you not remember our wild night of passionate lovemaking?" he asked. "Ah I'm deeply offended" he said as he put his hands over his heart and hung his head to one side.

He smiled as he went on, "you had one too many and fell asleep in the cab. I thought it was better to bring you here rather than leave you on your own at your place".

I broke down and cried. Gerry put his arm around me and said, "don't worry about it. Next time we'll go for dinner first and the booze won't go to your head".

Sitting on the tube on my way home later that day I thought about what a great guy Gerry was and what an idiot I was.

As the train noisily rumbled through the tunnels of the underground my inner voice was advising me on how to manage my drinking. Stopping drinking was never considered as an option.

I told myself that the positives of drinking massively outweighed the negatives as I listed the pros and cons in my head. Drinking allowed me to be someone who was normal and not a victim of abuse. It slowed down my thinking and took me outside of my own head for a while. It eased the pain and freed me from the constant sense of anxiety and dread I felt. Its only drawback was other peoples' perception of me when I drank too much.

As long as I did not get drunk in company everything would work out great. I was delighted that I had found the solution. I thought of the couple of tins of lager that were sitting in my fridge from the night before and decided to stop at the off licence for a few more, just to help me sleep.

Gerry and I did go out for a meal on the following

Tuesday night and I felt the need to apologise again for such a disastrous first date.

"I think I should keep a distance between myself and the Galtymore" I said jokingly. "The place definitely has a bad effect on me".

"Nothing to do with the 6 pints you had?" He asked.

"And I'd say you had more than one at your place before I got there".

I lied again, adamantly denying that I drank more than one.

"I'm taking it easy from now on" I said. "I'm not getting myself into that state again. A few drinks at 'staff afters' night and that's it".

"So, does that mean you're not coming out with me again? Or will you just not be drinking when we are on a date?" he asked.

I felt so comfortable with Gerry that I actually forgot that we were on a date!

When he reminded me, I became all flustered and schoolgirl like. I could feel my face going red and the hotter I got, the more embarrassed I became. I really liked Gerry, but I had no idea if I was going to be able to cope with our being anything more than friends. I was 22 years old and I had never been in an intimate, adult relationship.

I was so confused about how I felt about this because within myself, I felt so torn. One part of me wanted that unique feeling of being loved but I did not think that I was able to return that kind of love. I was also terrified of the physical aspect of intimacy. I did not know if the years of abuse had left me with permanent injury.

I thought about simply not going out with him again if he asked me but with that thought came feelings of disappointment and loss. My mind and my heart were in upheaval with thoughts and emotions that I could not control nor make sense of. I suddenly decided that the easiest way to deal with this was to leave my job in the Tarmon and not see Gerry again.

Once I decided to go, I wanted to hand in my notice immediately, yet I delayed in doing so because I knew that I would have to give a reason for leaving. I thought about just not turning up for work again, but I knew that Mary and Terry were likely to report me as a missing person to the police. I also thought that it would be unfair of me not to tell Gerry. As I pondered on what to do, I continued to go to work until Tuesday evening came around again.

Gerry and I were sitting outside a pub called "The Slug and Lettuce" in Richmond, looking into the Thames. Although it was summertime there was a cold chill blowing in from the river.

"What's going on with you?" Gerry asked. "You've been preoccupied about something all week".

I struggled with how to answer him, so I came out with the lamest of replies by saying, "nothing".

"Don't say 'nothing', I know somethings going on. Just tell me". He pleaded.

I thought about trying to explain but I had no idea where to start. I felt myself unwittingly take a deep breath and every nerve in my body started to jingle. My skin suddenly became clammy and I felt light-headed. I started to cry.

Gerry put his arm around me and gently asked me what had happened.

I told him.

"I was sexually abused when I was a child".

Neither of us said anything more. Gerry continued to

hold me, and I continued to let him.

I did not hand in my notice and for the next few weeks Gerry and I carried on dating. In that time, I told him about some of the abuse. He never asked me for any more than I wanted to say and never pressured me to continue with a conversation that I was uncomfortable with.

Chapter 5

In the Tarmon, the priority at the start of everyday was to get the pub ready for the lunchtime clientele and Thursday 18th June 1987 was no exception. As always Gerry would spend the morning cleaning and restocking the cellar while I concentrated on the bar. While I was doing the bottling up of the cold shelves, I could hear Terry calling me from the office at the top of the stairs, "Arl, phone call for you".

"Ok", I called back in reply.

As I made my way up the stairs, I struggled to think of anyone who might be calling me just after 9o'clock in the morning.

"Hello?", I said questioningly

The conversation that followed was the news that my whole family had been dreading for more than a decade. My brother, Keith, told me that Dad was in hospital in Dublin and the doctors said that he had not got long to live. I needed to get home as soon as possible. The next few hours passed in a bit of a haze as I tried to process the enormity of what was happening. I did not even know what to pack as I had no idea how long I might be at home. Neither had I any money for airfare or to live on while I was there. I sat down on the sofa in the sitting room and broke down. Once I started crying, I could not stop until finally I realised that Gerry was sitting beside me, rocking me like a baby in his arms.

"Terry has been on to Aer Lingus to book your ticket and Mary is packing your bag. Sit here for a while and then I'll book a cab to Heathrow".

"Gerry, I have no money for a ticket. What am I going to

do?" I could feel myself beginning to panic again.

"Terry insisted that he is paying, so don't worry about it. Do you want me to come with you?" he asked.

I thought for a brief moment and then replied, "No. Terry and Mary need you here. And I've no idea when I might be back. Jeez I don't even know where I'll be staying, never mind both of us. I'd rather go alone than have to think about all of that. Anyway, Dad could rally. He has defied the doctors this long. According to them we should have lost him years ago".

"Ok, but if you need me just ring the pub and I'll come over. Take this"

He handed me a wad of money.

"There's £300 there. If you need more ring the pub and I'll send it over. Terry got you booked on the next flight out, so we better call that cab."

I just nodded. I was completely overwhelmed with the kindness of these people. Neither they nor I knew if I was ever coming back, yet they had no hesitation in doing everything they could to help me.

Keith and Gavin were waiting for me at Dublin airport to bring me straight to the hospital. The car journey was sombre.

"Mum's in a bad way Arl", Gavin said.

"I suppose even after all these years nothing really prepares you when the time comes".

"He might pull through", I said hopefully. "He's done it before".

This time it was Keith who spoke. "Not this time".

Both Keith and Gavin reminded me so much of Dad but in entirely different ways. Gavin looked like him even though he did not have the dark colouring Dad had. Keith was more like him in his ways. They both had little to say most of the time but when they did speak it was often very poignant.

When we arrived at the hospital, we went straight to the relatives' room and the whole family were there. When I saw Cathy and Padraig my heart broke. They looked as though they had no idea what was happening but whatever it was, it was terrifying. Cathy was only 15 years old and Padraig not yet 12.

Mum looked exhausted which was not surprising when I learned that she had not left the hospital for the last two days. She was petrified of leaving in case Dad would pass away when she was not there.

"Can I see him?", I asked no one in particular.

Mum answered. "The nurse asked us to wait here for a few minutes while they made him more comfortable. We can go back in when they're done".

With that, a nurse put her head round the door to say that they were finished and that it was ok for us to go in. We all trooped into the ward where Dad was and because I had no idea about where I was going, I tagged along at the end of the line. There was also a part of me that was hesitant because I was afraid to find Dad in a bad way. There was a privacy screen around a patient at the far end of the ward and it was in this direction that everyone headed.

When we got there, Mum went in first and then the rest of us followed. I was surprised to see Dad sitting up and fully conscious. He was attached to an array of machines, all of which made a variety of sounds, but he was able to talk to us albeit with some difficulty, as he was wearing an oxygen mask. He tired very quickly though and after only a few minutes he appeared to have fallen asleep.

One of the nurses came in to check that he was ok and advised us to go for a rest or something to eat as he would be sleeping for the next couple of hours. By now it was late evening, so Keith asked everyone to go with him for something to eat and I stayed at the hospital with Mum.

By the time they all got back Dad was awake again, but it was very obvious that he was much weaker than he had been. He spoke to everyone again for a short while, but he tired much quicker this time. The nurses assured us that he was not in imminent danger so it was decided that it would be better if everyone went back to where they were staying for the night. Mum and I would stay in the relatives' room and if anything changed, we would contact them immediately.

The relatives' room had 4 long sofas that were used for sleeping on when people stayed at the hospital overnight. Mum and I lay down, both of us staring at the ceiling and saying very little. I do not know how long we were there when a nurse came in to tell us that Dad had taken a turn for the worse. When we got to the ward, most of the other patients were asleep so I guessed that it was quite late. Mum was by Dad's beside within seconds. When I walked behind the privacy screen Mum was leaning over the bed, holding Dad's head in her arms. As I stood there, I was unaware of how much time had passed until I heard a stranger's voice say, "he's gone".

As Mum continued to hold Dad, I felt like I was intruding so I stepped outside the screen and walked out of the ward to find a phone to ring the others.

My recollection of the next few days is snapshot images of each member of the family distraught and struggling to accept that Dad was really gone from our lives forever. He would never walk one of his daughters down the aisle or see his grandchildren grow up. He had not even celebrated his 50th birthday.

Dad had every detail of his funeral arranged. This forethought took a lot of pressure off Mum and the family. He had outlined a few things that he would like to be carried out. The undertaker, Sean Óg from Ballyshannon was to bring Dad home from Dublin in the hearse with the family in the cars behind. A group of men that worked with Dad over the years were going to join the procession in a variety of Carlton vehicles along the way.

One specific instruction from Dad was that the funeral procession be halted at the Derryagarra Inn in Butler's Bridge, Co. Cavan so that everyone could have a break on the long journey from Dublin to Donegal. He requested that he not be left alone outside so each one of Carlton's men took turns to stand by the hearse while the others enjoyed a drink inside.

On the morning of the funeral, the coffin was carried from the family home to the Rock Chapel. Padraig, in his confirmation suit, walking bravely behind is an image that I will never forget. The church was packed, so much so that many had to stand outside. It was Sunday 21st June 1987 which happened to be Father's Day, the final Father's Day for us, the Murphy children.

Over the next few days we each had to start making plans for returning to the lives we had temporarily left. This was very difficult because no one wanted to face the reality of having to leave Mum and Cathy and Padraig. For those of us living away from home Dad's passing would be more manageable on a daily basis but for them his absence in the home would be a constant reminder that he was no longer there.

Keith was living and working in Tyrone and Gavin in

Dublin and they had both taken as much time off from their jobs as they could. Michelle had been living and working in America and she too had to return to the life that she had there. I stayed at home for a couple of weeks and during that time I was in touch with Gerry every few days.

"Terry said that you should take as long as you need. Your job is waiting for you", he told me.

"I hate the thought of leaving Gerry but I'm not doing anything of any benefit either. Mum is devastated but she is getting on with it. Padraig is absolutely lost but at least he is out with his friends most times. Cathy has some really good friends too that are looking out for her. I know that Keith and Gavin will be home as often as they can, so I think it's time that I went back".

"If you're sure. Are you ok for money?"

"Terry got me an open return ticket that I can use anytime, and I still have some of the money you gave me. It will take me forever to work off what I owe".

"You don't owe me anything and I reckon that Terry would say the same. Let me know what flight you're on and I'll meet you at Heathrow".

"You don't have to", I said.

"I want to", he replied.

Going back to London was the right thing to do. We all needed to get on with our lives, as painful as that may have been. My hanging around at home was holding that up especially for Cathy and Padraig. Mum was dealing with things in her own way too and being there for her 2 young children was a part of that.

At times, being away from home made grieving more difficult while at other times it made it easier. I did not have the comfort of the people who were also grieving around me yet not having them there allowed me short gaps where I could almost forget that I was hurting so much. Working behind the bar and interacting with the customers allowed me to switch off my pain, as I listened to their worries and grievances.

The times that I struggled most was when I was alone. I knew that lying awake in bed, battling to get certain images out of my head, was going to be the worst, so I began bringing a large brandy to bed every night, just to help me to sleep.

Terry and Mary were fantastic. Even weeks after my return to work they refused to discuss the fact that I still owed them the cost of my return fare home, but I had a speech ready when my next payday came around. It was Mary handing out the wages on this occasion.

"Mary, I have to pay you and Terry back", I told her.

"I feel like I have a weight hanging over me and it's just adding to what's already going on for me".

"I didn't realise that love", she said with concern. "But Terry and I don't want you worrying about money".

"You guys are amazing and I'm so grateful. I couldn't pay you back in a lump sum but what if you took £20 out of my wages every week until I'd paid it off? I really would feel so much better just knowing that I was doing something".

"Ok, love", she agreed. "If that would be better for you, then we'll do that".

"It would Mary. Thank you so much".

As the summer was ending and autumn beginning, the tempo everywhere changed. The horde of tourists that had descended on the city lessened and stores that had advertised late night shopping closed their doors early. Local people on holiday went back to work and students returned to their schools and colleges. The old regulars of the Tarmon who had been away on holidays or those who were staying at home to spend time with their families returned to their usual seats and ordered their usual drinks. The pub was still as busy, but the pace slowed somehow. Terry let the temporary summer staff go and we all settled into a more mundane predictable routine.

Chapter 6

Wednesday 18th November 1987 started like so many other days but sadly ended with a tragedy that would never be forgotten. At about 7:30 that evening, Sean my driving instructor came into the Tarmon to pick me up for my weekly driving lesson, or so I thought. Instead, it was to tell us that King's Cross Station was on fire. Over the course of the night and the following day we learned some of the details of this horrific disaster.

The fire started on the Piccadilly line escalator going from the ticket hall down onto the train platform. A lit match was dropped and fell through a gap on the wooden escalator which set fire to the litter beneath the steps. The grease used to keep the escalators moving smoothly acted as an accelerant and the fire quickly burst into flames, trapping people who were alighting the still incoming trains below.

Fortunately, many passengers were able to escape using an alternative escalator and very quickly all the trains were instructed not to stop at the station. However, the fireball erupted back up as well as down and the ticket hall was still packed with the last of the rush hour commuters.

The intense heat in a confined space, forced firefighters to spray water over their colleagues in an attempt to keep the temperature bearable for brief periods of time, as they tried to rescue people. The molten plastic on the ceilings melted and dripped onto the people underneath and the thick smoke obscured the exits. People fell under the feet of others in their attempt to escape. It took more than 150 firefighters and 30 fire engines over 7½ hours to put out the blaze. By then 31 people had lost their lives and more than 100 others were injured.

One of those killed was a London firefighter, who witnesses later said, became engulfed as he tried to carry a passenger towards the steps leading to the St. Pancras Road exit of the station.

The King's Cross fire was reported to be the worst disaster in the history of the London Underground and the tragedy brought about many changes, which included replacing all the wooden escalators with metal ones. Following a fire at Oxford Station a few years previously smoking was banned on the trains but was permitted in other areas of the stations.

Within a week of the King's Cross fire it was announced that smoking was banned everywhere on London's public transport system.

Some people obviously found this new blanket ban to be too drastic and they continued to smoke on the platforms, out of sight of the London Underground staff. Fights regularly broke out as people attacked smokers for lighting up. It took some time for this no smoking ban to become the norm.

Parts of the station reopened within days of the fire, but the Piccadilly line remained closed for nearly 2 years. This made my journey in and out to work more difficult. The Caledonian road is almost 2 miles long from King's Cross to Holloway and although Holloway Station is on the Piccadilly line, the Tarmon is on the King's Cross side of the Cally. This meant that I would have to get a bus or a cab at night before catching my last train home. A cab every night was beyond my budget and having to rely on the bus to catch the train became a constant worry.

One day when Gerry and I were doing the lunchtime shift he suggested a solution, "move in to the Tarmon. I can ask Terry and Mary but I'm sure they'd be ok with it".

I did not immediately respond because I was unsure about what he was suggesting.

"What do you say?" he asked.

"Mmm don't know really".

"It would be perfect", he went on.

"There would be no more worries about having to leave early to catch the last train and Mary would take much less rent money than you are paying for that pokey wee bed-sit out in Bounds Green".

I felt myself going into a panic. My breathing became shallow and my body was tingling. I was sweating and struggling to find a response.

"Let me think about it", I said finally.

"What's to think about?", he asked.

"It's the perfect answer".

"I don't know if I'm ready for that Gerry".

He looked at me with a confused expression on his face and asked, "what do you mean?"

"Let's get this crowd fed and watered and we can chat later", I said as I walked away to serve a waiting customer.

For the next hour or so my head was in a spin, but I did my best to keep focus on the demanding lunchtime customers as they tried to make sure they had time to consume at least 3 pints of Murphy's stout and a bowl of Mary's mutton stew within the allotted one hour break.

As the frenzy of customers started to ease Gerry said that I could take my own lunchbreak. The very thought of eating was making me feel nauseous and I knew this was because I felt so anxious about the conversation we had earlier around my moving into the Tarmon so I said, "I'm ok yet. You have yours first". He needed no further persuasion.

"Ok I will, I've been looking at that stew and hoping

that it wasn't going to sell out before I got a bowl of it".

With that he strode behind the food counter and quickly scooped out a double portion of stew with all the trimmings.

"You'll never eat all that!" I stated incredulously.

"Watch me", he said with a big grin on his face.

Even with all the turmoil going on inside me Gerry could still make me smile.

Finally, the lunchtime crowd were gone, and Gerry and I had a few hours break. Terry took over the bar for the afternoon and Gerry went upstairs for his usual afternoon sleep between shifts. I would normally sit in the upstairs sitting room to watch TV or read a book.

Other times I would go shopping for any necessities I might need at home or I would stroll around King's Cross, taking in the atmosphere of real city life.

King's Cross was very different now. Although the parts of the station that were being used showed no evidence of there ever having been a fire, the smell was an obvious reminder. The ticket hall and the surrounding areas were revamped, and everything destroyed in the fire was replaced but the smell lingered.

And that was not all. There was a 'quietness' around the whole vicinity. Not just in the station itself but in the shops, in the restaurants and even in the bars around the area. The man selling papers at the news stand no longer made his presence known with the usual shout of "Standard!" the name of the city's newspaper. There were still the same amount of buses and taxis stopping to offload commuters and delaying for only a very short time as they refilled with more passengers outside the front of the station. The taxis that meandered around the various side streets looking for easier places to drop or pick up their fares did not seem to be fewer in number either.

The size of the crowd of people that usually milled around also appeared to be the same but there was, what looked like a 'slowing down' of sorts. No one rushed around. There was none of the familiar jostling for a place in the queues for the ticket machines, or the shouldering off one another to get in line for the single file turn-styles. It was eerie.

I was at a loss as to how to pass the afternoon.

I knew the topic of my living arrangements would come up again when I returned for my evening shift at the Tarmon but I did not want to think about that. I decided to go to The Skinner's Arms, a pub that Gerry had taken me to a few times. It was in Judd street which was very close by and it served food in the afternoons, which was why it could stay open. I had not eaten any lunch; in fact, I had not had breakfast either. I would be ravenous by the time I finished work tonight if I did not eat something now.

When I got there, I ordered a Ploughman's Lunch and a pint of lager. I did not often drink during the day and never between shifts, but I thought one drink with my lunch would be fine. I had already finished the pint when my food arrived, so I ordered another.

Before I knew it, I was ordering another drink and the Ploughman's was barely touched. I did not want to think about where my life was going because at that particular time, I was content with how things were. I felt so close to Gerry and I did not want that to change but I was aware that at some stage, our relationship would have to progress or cease. I was terrified at the prospect of either. Then Gerry walked in.

What I did not realise at the time, was that Gerry's arrival was hours later.

"Feck look at the cut of you!"

124

I tried to stand up, but I fell back down onto the seat that I had spent the afternoon on.

"What are you doing here?" I slurred

"And what time is it? I have to go to work".

"You had 6 pints of lager and then fell asleep. You've been out of it for more than an hour and the Gov'nor rang me when he couldn't wake you up. Look at the state of you! You can't work like that!"

In my drunken stupor I could not figure out if Gerry was angry or not. He had every right to be angry. I felt so ashamed of myself.

"What are we going to do?" he asked me. "Terry will go ape if he sees you".

"Tell him I'm sick and I'll just go home", I said.

"There is no way that you will get yourself to Bounds Green in that state. Do you think you could manage if I put you in a cab?" he offered.

"Yeah! No worries. I'll be sound," I said with a lot more confidence that I felt.

The truth was I felt so ashamed of myself that I just wanted to get out of there as quickly as possible. I was mortified as I noticed that everyone in the bar was watching and listening.

Gerry sat down and waited until the cab arrived. It was only a few minutes because it was already at King's Cross station waiting in the hope of a fare. But those few minutes felt like hours as Gerry sat in silence beside me.

At first the cab driver did not want to take me because he said he was afraid I would throw up in his car. I felt so embarrassed as Gerry tried to reassure him that I would not get sick and he looked at me for confirmation. I simply shook my head in reply, too ashamed to speak. The cab driver was still not convinced until Gerry offered him £20 on top of the fare, and another £10 if he vowed to see me safely inside my front door. Finally, he agreed, and I clamoured into the back of the cab very sheepishly.

"Sorry Gerry and thanks", I said as the car pulled away from the front of the pub. I could not even look back.

At 9:30 the next morning I was standing on the pavement outside the Tarmon. Shame and fear prevented me from ringing the bell. I did not know what to say to Terry about my not working my shift the evening before. I could hear Gerry moving barrels and kegs around in the cellar. I decided to wait until it went quiet.

That would mean that Gerry would be out of the cellar and behind the bar drawing up the settled ale through the beer lines as he checked to make sure that it was not cloudy.

I tapped on the public bar window.

Gerry's voice boomed a response. "We're not open yet! Come back in an hour!"

"Gerry its me. Let me in".

My stomach heaved as I heard the inside bolt of the public bar door being pulled back. Whether this was due to my hungover state or sheer anxiety I was not sure, but I suspect it was a huge pile of both. As I stepped over the threshold it was Terry's voice that greeted me and not Gerry's.

"Well I wasn't expecting you to show your face!".

Before I could say anything he went on, "are you sure that you are ok to work love? Gerry said that you got a dodgy prawn sandwich down round King's Cross and that you were in an awful state. You still look very pale you know. Go upstairs to Mary and have a bit of breakfast. See how you feel after that. Gerry and I can open up".

As I slowly walked towards the door to the private

living area I wondered where Gerry had gone. It was definitely his voice that shouted when I knocked on the public bar window. His head suddenly appeared over the counter. He was holding 3 bottles of tonic water in one hand and a cloth in the other. He had been stooped down, bottling up the mixers on the bottom shelf and said that he had been listening to what I was going to say to Terry. He was doing his best to stop himself from laughing out loud.

"Fair play to you for making it in though", he said. "I was telling Terry how sick you were yesterday, and I'd be surprised if you'd get here this morning. Feeling better, are you?"

Before I could answer Terry shouted from the other side of the bar.

"Some boyfriend he is! Imagine putting you in a cab home and you sick, instead of bringing you back here. Mary gave him a right rollicking for that!"

Right then, I really did not know whether I was going to laugh or cry! I was so relieved that I had not lost my job. But I also felt so ashamed. If Terry knew the real reason for my not showing up to work, he would have undoubtedly sacked me on the spot. Instead, he was full of concern for my well-being. He and Mary were so good to me and I was lying to them.

"Gerry, I feel terrible for lying to Terry".

His response was to laugh. "Well you can't tell him the truth!", he declared.

"Look, *chalk it up*", he said.

"Forget all about it and just get on with things. It was a bad idea to go on the beer when you had to work but lesson learned ok?"

"Yeah! Definitely!", I answered.

"Why did you do it anyway?", he asked.

127

"Can we talk about it later?". I knew that I would have to explain and wanted to do that without being interrupted by people coming and going in the bar.

"Let's go out for a meal when we finish tonight?" Gerry suggested. "I know a fantastic steak house in Hammersmith that caters for those of us in the pub trade. It stays open until about 4am. Will I ring them and book a table for 1am?"

"Yeah, great idea", I said.

For the rest of the day I could only think about the discussion that Gerry and I were going to have that night. I struggled with so much going around and around in my head. I really wanted to have a normal relationship and Gerry was fantastic. I knew that he cared a lot for me, and I felt safe with him but living together as a couple terrified me. I had no idea how I would manage being so close to another person in such an intimate way.

Suddenly, the ponderous and persistent one-way conversation in my head was over and Gerry and I were sitting in the back of a taxi on our way to Hammersmith. When we got to the restaurant Gerry wasted no time in getting to the point.

"Well, spill the beans", he said. Initially, I feigned ignorance, but I was not fooling anyone. I even tried stalling by insisting that we order our food first.

When I was all out of options I finally said, "I didn't mean to drink that much. I went into the Skinner's for some lunch. I really didn't intend to get drunk".

"So, what happened?" Gerry asked.

And the truthful answer was that I really did not know. When I was sober, I could convince myself that I could safely consume 2 or 3 drinks and then stop. But when I was worried about something and started drinking, I could not stop. For some reason that I was totally unaware of, I felt that I could not tell Gerry that.

Instead, I tailored the truth by saying, "I was thinking about what you had said about me moving into the Tarmon and I lost track of time".

"Well after all that thinking what did you come up with?", he asked.

"I don't know Gerry. I've never lived with anyone before".

The look on his face spoke volumes! And without him having to say another word I realised that I had totally misunderstood the whole situation.

I was mortified. It was difficult to ascertain which of us was the more embarrassed. And then Gerry did what he always did, he started to laugh. And then so did I.

"I was all up in knots about us living together and that's not what you meant when you suggested I move into the Tarmon was it?"

"Well, no it wasn't. I thought maybe you could rent Rodney's room. That's the one you are usually in when you stay over."

Rodney was Mary and Terry's nephew. He was a student in Dublin and came over to London whenever he could. He was studying engineering in UCD and stayed in the Tarmon when he was on a break from college. Terry was co-owner of an engineering company in Wembley Park and Rodney did his work experience there.

"Rodney might not be too pleased when he next arrives at the Tarmon to find his room permanently occupied", I stated.

"Look there's no harm in chatting to Mary and Terry about it, is there?"

"Suppose not. It would cut out all the hassle travelling over and back to Bounds Green, not to mention how much money I'd save. I don't know though…."

"Look you can only ask and if they say no its no big deal. Ok?"

"OK", I said. "I'll ask Mary tomorrow when I'm on afternoon break".

"Yeah. Stay out of the Skinner's," he smirked.

"Stop!", I pleaded. "I'm never setting foot in that place again.

That was the last mention of my *'afternoon debacle'* in the Skinner's Arms.

I need not have had any worries about asking to 'live in' in the Tarmon. When I broached the subject with Mary she was delighted.

"It will be fantastic to have another woman in the house", she said.

Initially Mary jumped to the same conclusion that I had and mistakenly thought that I would be moving into Gerry's room. When I explained that I wanted to rent Rodney's room her enthusiasm remained the same.

"Makes no odds, whatsoever", she said. "We can have girlie nights in".

She went on to say that when Rodney visited, he could bunk down on the sofa in the sitting room. Apparently, he was in his last year at college and when he qualified, he would be taking a year out to go travelling before he settled into full-time employment. That would mean that the room was going to be empty so my moving in was not going to cause any great upheaval.

I was absolutely thrilled, and I could not wait to give notice to my landlord in Bounds Green. When the time came for my moving out Gerry had it all organised. A friend of his called Brian was a painter and decorator and Brian used a small van for his work. Gerry had arranged for Brian to have his van empty so that there would be room for my stuff. The plan was that I would move out on the last Sunday of the month when neither Brian, Gerry nor I would be working.

It did not take long to load my stuff into the van because there was so little of it. I had accumulated little or nothing because there was no room for any extras in such a tiny bed-sit. Therefore, with only a couple of bags of clothes and a hold-all of nick-knacks there was loads of empty space in the van. So much so, that I chose to sit in the back on the journey back to the Cally.

I loved living in the Tarmon. Being there was like being part of a family. Gerry and I continued to date so when the locals heard that I had moved into the pub they assumed that Gerry and I were living together as a couple. We never bothered to make them any the wiser, but Gerry was forever the gentleman and when we were together, he never tried to manipulate or coerce me into a situation that I might be uncomfortable with.

The more time I spent with him the more I grew to love and trust him. On many an occasion we spent the night together, talking and holding each other until we fell asleep. Over time our relationship did evolve and for the first time in my life I thought that maybe, just maybe, I could live my life just like everyone else.

Chapter 7

Gerry and I were preparing the bar for opening on a typical Monday morning. The cellar was done, bottling up finished and the tables in the saloon bar laid for lunch. At the strike of 11 Gerry drew back the bolt on the door and in walked a brewery rep.

"Wow! You're on the ball", Gerry said.

"Arl will you be ok for a while?"

"Yeah no problem", I replied.

It was part of Gerry's job as manager to talk to all the reps. from the different breweries. He would tell them what was selling well and what was not, and they would be offering promotions to encourage him to take on one of their products in place of a similar one from another brewery. These negotiations would sometimes be over very quickly while at other times they could go on for up to an hour. This was a lengthy stint. When the rep finally left Gerry came back behind the bar and we started to gear up for the onslaught of hungry and thirsty navvies due in from the new construction site on Bingfield Street, which was just walking distance from the Tarmon.

The lunchtime session was manic what with someone shouting for a pint of Guinness on one side of the bar and someone else shouting for bowl of stew on the other. I was in my element and loved the mayhem of dashing from one customer to another, usually serving 2 or 3 at the same time. From 1 o'clock until 2 o'clock there was no let up and then suddenly as though someone shouted *'fire!'* the place emptied. Anyone would have thought that Gerry and I had been holding our breath for the hour as we both audibly exhaled in unison.

We looked around and saw the deluge of destruction the navvies had left in their wake and Gerry said, "lets have a drink and a fag before we start into clearing up this lot!".

There was no argument from me.

"What do you want to drink?" he asked.

"Diet coke", I said.

I had decided to avoid drinking in the afternoons especially when I was working.

When Gerry had his own drink and was sitting down beside me, he suddenly said, "How would you like to be a landlady?"

"Huh?", I asked stupidly.

"What do you mean?"

"That rep this morning, he was from Charrington's Brewery".

I waited for him to go on.

"He said they are looking for a couple to manage one of their pubs up in the Elephant & Castle. He wondered if you and I might be interested in going for it".

"What did you tell him?"

"Well, I said 'Yeah' but I'd have to run it by you"

"So, you told him 'Yes' didn't you?" I said in a kind of a panicked high pitch.

"Shush!" Gerry said holding his finger to his lips.

"I don't want Terry and Mary to know until we decide".

I could see how excited Gerry was. Although he was the manager in the Tarmon I knew that he was doing all the work without really being able to reap the benefits.

That was because the Gov'nor, Terry lived on the premises as it was a *free house*. If Gerry got a brewery pub his position as manager would make him the Gov'nor, only answerable to a brewery area manager.

"Let's go out later and talk about it", he suggested.

"I'll ring the steakhouse and book a table. We better start into sorting this place out or the Monday Club will complain about the mess. Although it would be a cheek, seeing as they are getting a *lock-in*."

My mind was in turmoil as I scraped plates and loaded glasses into the washer. These past months had been bliss, and I was hesitant to change that. I never really considered that Gerry might want to move on but in hindsight it was inevitable that he would want his own pub someday. I certainly could not stand in his way.

Come midnight we were sitting in what had become our usual table in the steakhouse in Hammersmith. No sooner had we ordered our food and drinks when Gerry asked, "Well, do you want to live in the Elephant?"

Instantly, I replied "Yeah!"

Gerry was over the moon. He immediately started to tell me all about it.

"The pub is called the Tankard and it's on the Walworth road. It's a small place and the clientele are *suits* what with Labour Party HQ right next door. We'll miss the Irish lads, but we won't be scraping cement off the floor either!"

The decision was made and the next morning Gerry rang the brewery to say that we were interested in the job. We decided that it would be best not to say anything to Terry and Mary for the time being, just in case we changed our minds. Gerry arranged for us to go and see the Tankard that afternoon. When we arrived at the agreed time the rep that there to meet us.

Within minutes Gerry said, "I can see meself behind that bar!"

After having a good look around downstairs, I was keen to see the living quarters. Although it was an old building, it had all the *mod cons* and like Gerry, I too could see myself living there.

We sat down with the rep to discuss our moving in. It was currently under temporary management by a single man and he would remain there until Gerry and I worked out our notice in the Tarmon. That meant that we would not be leaving Terry and Mary in the lurch over Christmas, but we would be gone before the New Year. The thought of telling them that we were leaving made me so anxious I would have done almost anything to avoid having to do it. Gerry, as usual, saw only the bright side.

"They'll be delighted for us", he said.

And he was right. Mary was so happy for us that she initially began to cry and then started discussing plans for our leaving party. Instead of working out a month notice, Terry asked us to stay just long enough for him to get a full-time bar/cellar man. They wished us well for our future and even gave us both a bonus on top of our due holiday pay.

Within a fortnight we had moved into the Tankard. It was very strange at first, but it did not take us long to get to know the regulars and their quirks. In the Tarmon the daytime customer was also the night customer but in the Tankard the clientele and what they drank changed with the hands on the clock.

Before 7pm we served lunch to businessmen. They drank half a pint of real ale with their Ploughman's while their female counterparts drank a glass of dry white wine with their Caesar salad. After 7pm our customers were local residents, living in the tower blocks at Heygate or in small apartments up and down the Walworth road from Southwark to

Camberwell. Our male night-time customers drank pints of bitter and lager with whiskey and dark rum chasers while the ladies preferred a bottle of Holsten Pils or a Cinzano with lemonade. It was like running two very separate pubs. We fell in love with the Tankard and all its clientele almost instantly. They too welcomed us and before long we had made it our home.

We both worked really hard to make the business a success and within the first 6 months the takings had more than doubled. With success came freedom as the area manager's visits became less frequent. The brewery carried out a regular 3-month stock take and this was the only time we saw anyone resembling a boss.

The brewery gave us the go ahead to employ a full-time bar person and although this took a lot of pressure off us, Gerry and I still covered almost every shift except for a Tuesday night when we went out for a meal together. Gerry always said that the secret to running a good pub was to have the Gov'nor and the Landlady around the bar a lot of the time and this was certainly proving to be true.

When we did go out, we usually stayed local and returned to the Tankard before last orders. It became routine that we served after hours drinks on a Tuesday night but only for a select few. The regulars would be given a secret invite to stay behind while unknown customers *were allowed* to leave.

Serving after hours on an afternoon, the way we did in the Tarmon, would have been impossible because the Tankard was right in the middle of a busy area, surrounded by shops and offices. Within 100 yards were the offices of the Metropolitan Police Forensic Unit. Much of the staff there came to us for lunch and were often not in a great hurry back to work which would have made an afternoon illegal lock-in out of the question. Tuesday night became the Tankard's version of a Monday club and just like in the Tarmon, its members were very exclusive.

What began as a typical Tuesday ended as an especially memorable one for me in May 1988. That morning Gerry informed me that instead of us taking our usual night off we were taking the whole day off.

"Why?" I asked. "Where are we going?"

"Never mind. Just be ready by 2pm. A cab is coming to pick us up and you'll find out then".

I was so excited and could not think of anything specific that Gerry could have planned. My 23rd birthday was earlier in the month and Gerry had spoiled me for the whole day. I woke up to breakfast in bed and a massive card with *'happy birthday to the girl I love'* written on the front accompanied by 23 red roses. The day ended with Gerry bringing me to see a show in the city followed by a beautiful meal in China Town.

I searched my mind and felt confident that there was no anniversary or significant date that we should be celebrating. I finally gave up trying to guess what he was up to and decided to just enjoy the rare event of having a full day off together.

When the cab arrived, I eagerly jumped into the back seat and Gerry got in beside me. He instructed the driver to go towards Holborn. Although I had told myself that I would not subject myself to the torture of trying to figure out why Gerry was being so mysterious, I could not stop the array of possibilities going around in my head. *'Going towards Holborn'* was a snippet of information that was frustratingly worthless because it did not fit, in any form, into any of the scenarios that I had conjured up.

It seemed that whatever was going on, I would not be made privy to it until the very last minute.

After about half an hour Gerry asked the cab driver to stop. He paid the fare and we both got out. I had no idea where we were, but it was very obvious that Gerry knew exactly where he was and where he wanted to go. Without saying a word, he took my hand and steered me down a narrow street. He suddenly stopped outside a small black wooden door and rang what I thought was a doorbell. I could hear a buzzing sound from inside followed by a loud click. Gerry pushed the door open and stepped inside with me in his wake. We were standing in a jewellery shop.

An elderly gentleman came around from behind the counter saying, "welcome to Flaxman's of Hatton Garden".

He shook Gerry's hand and said, "follow me". He led us to a small room behind the counter and indicated for us to go inside. He then closed the door behind us. The room was empty except for a small table with 2 glasses of Buck's Fizz and a vase of flowers on it. Gerry had not uttered a word since getting out of the cab. He got down on one knee, held my hand and said, "marry me". I was stunned.

Stupidly I asked, "Is that a question?"

"Yeah it is! Will you marry me?" When I looked into Gerry's eyes, I saw love looking back at me.

I did not hesitate. "Yes, I will".

We went out into the shop to choose the ring.

The second I saw it I knew it was the right one, a sapphire surrounded by 6 small diamonds. Gerry put it on my finger, and it was a perfect fit.

All my life I believed that I would never marry. I always thought that the sexual abuse in my childhood excluded me from having an intimate relationship with anyone. Gerry changed all that with his patience and understanding. He gave me the time and the space to deal with things in my own way and always made me feel comfortable and safe.

When we got back to the Tankard that evening there was a big crowd waiting for us. Gerry's brother Martin and his sister Joanne and her husband Roy were there as well as Terry and Mary and a few regulars from the Tarmon. We celebrated into the early hours and as usual, because I had been drinking, I had no memory of how or when the night ended.

Life seemed perfect but a part of me always felt uneasy or unsettled. I could not understand why I still felt this way. I knew I loved Gerry and the life we were living, yet I could not convince myself that I was truly happy. Gerry had mentioned several times that he was concerned about how I was drinking. For a month or more, I would drink no alcohol whatsoever but then when I started, I would drink almost constantly for a couple of days. Although at these times I would be drinking throughout the day I had learned how to function and to keep up appearances. It was when the pub closed at night that I would sit alone and just get drunk.

Gerry had asked me many times what was going on for me, but I could not give him any answers. I could only respond with 'I don't know'. He said that he had mentioned his worries about me to his sister, Joanne, and she thought that I may be struggling with bouts of depression. Gerry was very close to his older sister and I was glad that he was able to talk with her, even though I was not entirely happy about not being there when they were having this conversation. I liked Joanne and I knew that any input from her would have been well meant.

"Joanne said if you want a chat with her on your own that you could call round to her place anytime", Gerry said.

"I appreciate that Gerry but if I do have depression

wouldn't it better to just go to the doctor?"

"If you like I'll come with you?" he offered.

"Yeah, I'd like you to be there", I replied.

We went together to the first available appointment the following day. I struggled to find the words to explain how I felt sitting in the waiting room. I could only equate it with how a child might feel sitting outside the headmistress's office because they had done something naughty. When my name was called, I wanted to run out of the building, and go anywhere except into the doctor's office.

Gerry had told me that he had explained the nature of our visit when he made the appointment, and this went a long way in putting me at ease. I had always insisted in having a female GP which also helped.

Dr. Majella Harkin was, I guessed, in her 50's. She invited us to sit down and spoke directly to me in a very sensitive and non-judgemental manner.

"Good afternoon Arylene. What can I do for you today?"

I looked at her but could not answer.

"When your partner Gerry made the appointment, he said that you were both worried about your drinking. Is that right?"

"Yes", I mumbled.

"Before we talk about that I'd like to do a quick check-up. Is that ok?"

"Yeah, sure". I sighed with relief.

She took my blood pressure, listened to my chest and looked into my ears, eyes and throat. She then asked me to lie on the examination table.

She felt around my tummy and asked me to return to my seat.

I started to feel anxious. I knew we had to discuss the reason we were there but in a million years, I never would have guessed the words she next uttered.

"Do you know that you are pregnant?"

I was unable to speak. My mind shut down and I disconnected. I heard Gerry voice his astonishment and then his joy.

He put his arms around me saying, "that's fantastic news! Me, a Dad. I don't believe it!"

At that moment I felt nothing. It was as though I was not even in the room. My lack of response seemed to be a concern for the doctor. I heard her ask me if I was ok. She said that my reaction was not uncommon when a baby was not planned. I was in shock.

"What do we do now Doc?" I heard Gerry ask.

"By my examination I think the pregnancy is 5 to 6 months on. We need to get Arylene into pre-natal care immediately".

I was suddenly back in the room and in a state of panic.

"What have I done? The drinking...have I hurt the baby?"

Dr. Harkin replied, "you didn't know about the baby, but you must stop now. I'll make an emergency appointment for you to see someone who can help. Will you talk to someone if I do that?"

"Yes. Definitely". I vowed.

When Gerry and I got back to the Tankard he wanted to share the news with everyone.

"Before we tell anyone I have to tell my Mum! She hasn't even met you! I don't know how she'll take it". I was more than a bit worried.

"She'll be fine", he said. "She was ok with us getting

141

engaged".

"Feck's sake, Gerry! This is obviously a much bigger thing. Dad only died last year and now this! Being pregnant and not married is a really big deal in Ireland. They still have those feckin' Magdalene Mother & Baby Homes so it shows far behind things are over there! I know that Mum is pretty cool about most things, but this is a worry she doesn't need. We're supposed to be going home in a couple of months for Michelle's wedding. By then I'll be 7 or 8 months and bound to be showing! I'm supposed to be singing in the chapel! We'll have to tell Michelle we can't go!"

"Calm down! Let's take it one step at a time. We'll phone your Mum tonight".

"What are we waiting for? Let's just ring her now".

I started to dial the number, stopped and hung up.

I suddenly remembered something that happened many years before. A good friend of mine in school discovered she was pregnant and was terrified to tell her Mum and Dad. She said that she would prefer to talk to my Mum first.

She was only 16 years old and frantic with worry, but Mum reassured her that everything would work out. And, of course, it did.

Mum has always been more broad-minded than most and never worried about 'what the neighbours thought'. With this in mind, I dialled the number again and this time I waited for Mum to pick up.

We chatted for a long time. Her resounding message was if I was happy then she was. She did ask a couple of very obvious questions that I had not even thought of, the main one being 'how did I not know that I was pregnant?' The only answer to that was it was a result of my drinking, but I did not want to tell her that as it would only add to her concerns. I went through so many emotions during that phone call as I have no doubt Mum did. I felt so guilty because I believed that I had disappointed her, and I had brought shame on the family.

Mum was very adamant that I had no reason to feel that way because it simply was not true. She did go on to say that she would have preferred that Gerry and I were married but it was entirely our decision about what we should do. She ended the conversation by saying that she wanted us to come home in July for Michelle's wedding as planned. She even agreed to tell everyone at home about *my condition* before my arrival to save me any embarrassment.

My next phone call had to be to Michelle and although I knew that Mum would be talking with her, I felt that I needed to speak with her myself. So, rather than put it off, I rang her straight away. She picked up on the second ring.

"Hey sis, how you?" came her chirpy voice.

I thought it best to just delve in. "I have something to tell you".

"No way! Do <u>not</u> tell me that you are not coming home for the wedding?!"

"Well, you might not want me there when I tell you what's happening" I said.

I waited for her response and when it finally came, she asked, "what are you on about? Of course I want you there, you're singing aren't you?"

"That's just it though, you might not want me to". I knew what I was saying was not making any sense to her so before she could speak again, I blurted out, "I'm pregnant".

There was silence on the other end of the phone. I grew more and more anxious as I waited for her response. When it came, I was overwhelmed with emotion as I realised that she was more concerned than angry.

"Are you ok Arl?" she asked.

I could not answer for a minute. When I did speak the words caught in my throat.

"Yeah I'm ok, but it's absolutely fine if you don't want us to come to the wedding".

"Of course you guys are coming but did you speak to Mum?"

"Just a few minutes ago. I think she's ok. She said that we should come home as planned".

"Then it's sorted", she said.

"It's probably best if I don't sing though? I'll be 7 or 8 months on and I don't want to make a show of you on your special day".

The phone was silent again.

"You still there?", I asked.

"How come you're only telling us now sis?"

"I didn't know until today! I went to the doctor for something else and she told me I was about 5, maybe 6 months pregnant. I think I'm still in shock".

"I could ask you a hundred questions, but I won't even start. Are you and Gerry ok with it? As long as you guys are happy then get on with it. And I still want you to sing if you are up for it?" She started to chuckle then and added, "we'll give the old gossips something to chew on!"

The reality of the situation began to sink in over the next few days for me. Gerry was so excited that it was nearly impossible to get him to discuss any practicalities for the future. We did talk about whether we should get married in a registry office before the baby was born but neither of us was really keen on that idea. We wanted our wedding to be a big

144

Irish fanfare, at home with our families.

I was worried about our jobs as managers in the Tankard, but the brewery dispelled that instantly. They believed that the arrival of a baby would ensure our commitment to a long-term contract and they were very happy about that. With all the major issues dealt with I was finally able to become more excited about the baby myself. I still had a lot of fears, not least of all the prospect of giving birth. In the pre-natal classes I learned that a first baby could take a couple of days to arrive after the mother first began to have contractions. I was terrified but I tried to remind myself that Mum always used to say that we girls would probably be just like her in that she always had a short labour, including her first.

By the time we were due to go home for the wedding my tummy was massive. Apparently, this was not an uncommon phenomenon among woman who discovered their pregnancy late on. Although I had been talking to Mum and Michelle regularly, I was becoming more and more worried about how my family would react when they saw me. It was one thing to talk about being pregnant but the reality of seeing me might be another.

When we arrived in Ballyshannon, we were greeted with love and acceptance from everyone. My brothers Keith and Gavin said that were solely disappointed to discover that we got to Mum's before them as they had planned a special welcome for Gerry. They were going to play a joke on him. They had decided to be waiting on the doorstep, each of them holding one of Dad's guns, Keith the shotgun and Gavin the rifle. This was in reference to a *shotgun wedding*. Gerry would have found it very funny once he got over the fright!

Michelle's wedding went without a hitch and all too

quickly it was time for Gerry and me to return to London. As always, it was difficult to say goodbye, but we had already decided that we would be home again before Christmas, and we would have the baby with us.

When we got back to the Tankard, I felt so happy and finally at ease. Seeing my family took away all my worries. Over the following weeks my tummy grew larger and my pre-natal check-ups showed that everything was well, both with myself and the baby. I suffered none of the common ailments that expectant mothers often had to deal with and felt very grateful for that. I did not even develop any food cravings, strange or otherwise and apart from my enlarged tummy my body showed no other signs of pregnancy.

However, my mind and my heart showed plenty. I was so happy that I found it impossible to describe. I could not believe that I was actually having my very own baby. It was beyond my wildest dreams. I felt an overwhelming protectiveness and I did everything to ensure the safety of the baby inside me.

One Sunday evening I suddenly felt an ache in my lower back. As evening turned into night the ache became more intense. Although I never had this ache before I thought perhaps it might just be the weight I was carrying at the front. I decided to have a hot bath in the hope that a long soak would ease the nagging pain.

Sunday was early closing in the pub trade and by the time Gerry had finished in the bar it was coming up to 11:30pm. When he came upstairs to the sitting room, he found me lying on the sofa in a lot of discomfort. Gerry decided to phone the hospital where I was due to have the baby just to check that there was nothing wrong and we were both very relieved to discover that my symptoms were perfectly normal in the last stage of a pregnancy.

However, over the next few of hours the pain became even more intense and I just knew that I was in labour and that we should go to the hospital. Gerry rang an ambulance and by the time we arrived at the accident and emergency department of Guy's Hospital it was 2:30am. On Monday, 15th August 1988 at 4:31am we had a beautiful baby girl. She weighed 6 pounds and 2 ounces, was 19 inches long and she was 100% healthy. She was perfect.

Until that moment I knew that I had never known how happy a person could be. I had never known such joy nor such peace. From the second I held her I knew that my life was now hers and nothing else in the world mattered more.

On the following Wednesday afternoon, we were discharged from hospital, and Gerry and I could not wait to bring our little girl home. He carried her around in his arms, introducing her and to every punter that came through the door.

"This is my daughter, Siobhán", he'd say proudly.

Most of our clientele were unfamiliar with the Irish name and when Gerry spelled it out it was even more confusing as its pronunciation did not match the spelling. Everyone said that she was his image which delighted him even more.

Over the weeks she thrived, growing stronger and more alert with every passing day. Gerry was a fantastic Dad and took every opportunity to change her, bathe her and dress her. He could not do the night feeds because I was nursing her, but he rose when I did and took over as soon as she was fed. He carried her over his shoulder until she burped and then he changed an often very stinky nappy and carried her again until she fell asleep in his arms. She was a very happy baby and the customers often remarked that no one would ever know that there was a baby in the house because she so seldom cried. On the occasions when she did cry, she was easily pacified.

When she was one month old, we brought her to Southwark registry office to register her birth. Her full name was Siobhán Marie O'Reilly. We choose Siobhán because both of us really liked the name and picked Marie as her second name after my Mum. Although Gerry and I were unmarried we could register Siobhán using Gerry's surname because he was present at the time of the registration. We both wanted to have her baptized and decided that we would like to do that in my parish, in Donegal. After making enquiries we discovered that that would not be issue and so planned her christening for the time we were due to go home.

We decided that we would spend our first family Christmas in Ireland with our own families and so arranged with the brewery to have more than a month off. As I had not taken any maternity leave, they were very happy to accommodate us. Temporary managers would take over from 2nd December until our return on 4rd January.

Everyone back home was so keen to meet the latest addition to both the Murphy family and the O'Reilly one. Arranging her christening to coincide with our visit meant that both families would be there. We chose Gerry's brother, Martin to be Godfather and Cathy, my sister as Godmother.

For the next couple of months, I wallowed in motherhood. I loved having Siobhán with me all the time. I felt a little lost when I had to put her into her Moses basket to sleep. I talked to her when she was awake and sang to her when she was falling asleep. I never wanted to leave her. I constantly promised her that I would never let anyone hurt her the way I had been hurt as a child. I knew I was being over-protective, but I told myself that in time I would settle down.

When she was about 3 months old, I had to stop nursing her because she was never getting enough to satisfy her hunger. She started having solid food and a bottle of formula which suited her much better. This however gave me free reign to begin drinking again. I told myself that a few drinks now and again would do harm.

Finally, the time had arrived for our trip home. We had packed Siobhán's gifts from Santa and made sure that we had all the correct paperwork for her christening. A few of my family were not sure when they would arrive over the holidays so we were waiting to book an exact date until we saw the parish priest to agree a date that would suit everyone. Given that we were going to be there for over a month we could not foresee any issue with that.

On Friday 3rd of December we travelled from the Elephant & Castle to Heathrow airport. The Aer Lingus staff were told in advance that a baby would be on the flight and they did everything possible to ensure that Siobhán was comfortable and safe. She was strapped to me for the entire journey and she slept through it. When we arrived in Dublin, Gerry's brother in law, Ray was waiting to bring us to Ballyshannon. As we covered mile after mile, Siobhán continued to sleep and I grew more and more excited. When we crossed the border at Belleek, she finally awoke. It was, as though she knew that we were nearly home.

When the car came to a stop outside our family home at number 12 East Rock, my youngest brother Padraig was the first to come running out. My heart broke when I caught a glimpse of him. I had not seen him since Dad's funeral last year. He was only 12 years old and he had already suffered such a terrible loss. He and Dad were extremely close. They spent every possible minute together, fishing, shooting or stuck under the bonnet of an old car. On days when Dad was feeling up to it, they could both be found in Carlton's quarry or around the garage in Sligo. One sure bet was that wherever they were, if school was out, they were together.

"Hey Arl, show us the baby", he shouted as he ran towards us.

You would imagine that a 12-year-old boy would have little interest in a baby, but he could not wait for me to take her out of the car.

"Do you want to hold her?" I asked and without any hesitation he took her gently in his arms and carried her into the house. As I walked a few steps in behind him, I heard him say, "I'm your Uncle Padraig".

Everyone made a big fuss of Siobhán and she loved it. There were so many gifts for her that we would never be able to bring them all back to London. She did not make shy with anyone and was very happy to be lifted and passed around from uncle to aunt and finally to Granny. I was not nursing her all the time now and she was very content to allow her Granny to give her a bowl of rice followed by a bottle of milk. Fed and changed she was ready for another nap.

While she was sleeping Gerry and I took the opportunity to go to the priest's house on the off chance he would be in. Now that we were home, we thought that we could discuss a date for the christening and then check with everyone if it suited. It was a short walk away and as we neared the house, we noticed that there were lights on. Of course, that was no guarantee that the priest was home, only that the housekeeper was. As luck would have it, he was home as he opened the door to us himself.

After welcoming us in and our declining the offer of tea, we told him who we were and why we were there. He said that he was delighted that we had decided to have Siobhán baptized in my home parish and given the amount of time that we were going to be around for, we would have a number of dates to choose from. We offered him the paperwork regarding Siobhán's birth and registration. He read it in silence and then stated, "you are not married".

I guess because Siobhán had Gerry's surname he assumed that we were married.

"Is that a problem Father?", Gerry asked.

"Well, we would prefer to baptize children born into the sanctity of Holy Marriage," he answered pompously.

"Really!" Gerry said.

It was quite obvious by his tone that he was getting angry. "Is that a rule then? Are you saying that you won't baptize our child? Is that what you're saying?"

"No, not at all. I'm just saying that it would be better, that's all", the priest stammered.

"We are making plans to marry Father", I offered. "But it could be year or two".

The priest turned to me saying, "maybe wait to have the christening then?"

"No!", I wailed. "We don't want to wait! It's important that she is baptized".

Gerry stood up and towering over the priest he said, "If you won't do it, we'll have her baptized back in London. Priests over there are not stuck in the dark ages".

"Hold on, Mr.O'Reilly, I did not say that I would not do it. I just need to check that the paperwork is in order. Allow me to photocopy these documents and I will get in touch with you as soon as possible. Is that ok?"

Gerry nodded and the priest left the room.

"Smarmy bastard!" Gerry muttered. I had never seen him so angry before.

I was devastated. All the excitement was now tainted. And we did not know for sure that there was even going to be a christening. Whatever was said between the priest and Gerry after that was lost on me.

Gerry and I walked back to Mum's house on that Friday night in silence.

I do not clearly remember the conversation we had when we got there but I do remember Mum trying to calm us both down.

"He never said that he wouldn't do it", she stated, which was of course true. "There are some priests that will not baptize babies outside of marriage and I think that the rules still. But a lot of them ignore the old rules. Maybe he's one of them".

"I hope so Mum. But it didn't sound like it to me".

I went upstairs and Siobhán was sleeping soundly in her cot. My heart ached as I watched her. I felt that she had been rejected. My beautiful little girl turned away, not good enough, because of some stupid rule.

I went back downstairs and said to Gerry, "open that bottle of vodka you got you in the Duty Free. Let's celebrate being home and forget about the bloody priest!" That is my last memory of that night.

I woke the following morning with Siobhán in the bed beside me. I lifted her. She was limp. I could not wake her. I started screaming.

Mum came running into the room and took her from me.

"Wake her up Mum", I screamed.

Mum sat down on the bed and started to rock my baby girl. She was kissing the top of Siobhán's head and gently rocking her as though she was sleeping. For a brief second I thought she was sleeping, then a stabbing pain pierced my chest and I started screaming again.

I have only vague flashbacks of events after that.

Siobhán lying in too large a bed in a side ward in the Sheil Hospital. Gerry crying tears of heartache as he refused to allow the priest into the room. Mum holding her as we travelled in the back of an ambulance to Sligo. People I did not know asking lots of questions. Keith carrying a tiny white coffin because Gerry could not do it. Mum's long, red winter coat coming in and out of my peripheral vision as it blew in the wind while we stood by the graveside. Lowering my precious baby down into a deep dark hole. Our beautiful little girl, only 4 months old, gone forever. My now silent screams eliminated all sound outside of me as I surrendered to the brokenness within me.

Chapter 8

Within a week we had the results of the post-mortem. We lost Siobhán to SIDS, sudden infant death syndrome or cot death as its more familiarly known. Although I had been torturing myself with thoughts of my having smothered her as I lay in a drunken stupor alongside her, the findings of the post-mortem did little to alleviate any guilt.

Neither did it give us any real explanation as to why she died. We desperately needed an answer, a medical diagnosis to what had killed our baby, but we got none. We were told that there were none. Our beautiful baby girl who was in perfect health simply died for no reason.

We were officially informed that Siobhán had a full stomach and a dry nappy which proved that she had been fed and changed shortly before she died. Padraig told me that he had seen me do that when he got up to use the bathroom in the early hours, but I had no recollection of that. The last hours I shared with her were lost in a drunken blackout. Nothing could ever ease the shame of that.

Gerry found the idea of having to return to London without her totally inconceivable although staying in Ireland without her was every bit as incomprehensible. He was so devastated it seemed that nowhere on this earth could possibly be hospitable. It was totally unfeasible for me to support him in his grief because my own was so overwhelming. I struggled to even be near him because the guilt I felt was so totally encompassing. I had let him down in the most despicable way and deserved all the contempt he should have had for me.

He continuously tried to reassure me by saying that he

did in no way hold me responsible for our daughter's death, but I did not believe him. How could he not blame me? Had I not been drunk I surely would have noticed that there was something terribly wrong. Not being able to remember the last precious hours that I had spent with Siobhán was a betrayal to him and to her. How could he forgive me for abandoning our child?

The feelings of pain and loss were indescribable. I felt that a huge part of me was missing. There was an emptiness inside of me that nothing could ever fill. People always say that *'time is a great healer'* but I knew that regardless of time, this state of loss was now innate. Nothing could heal the bond that was now broken.

When we got back to work the customers in the Tankard asked us where she was. That went on for weeks. Gerry was able to manage this better than I and in time he seemed to take refuge in the job. He worked every shift, even the ones he did not have to and focused all his attention on building the business. This was largely due; I believe to my unavailability to him or to the work.

My only focus, if one could call it that, was to drink as much and as often as I could. Initially I feigned some kind of interest in believing that life could go on, but very quickly I lost the motivation to even pretend.

Most days I presented myself as the landlady by donning the outfit and putting on the *face*. I hid my drinking during the day and lied that the vodka and coke I poured at 7pm was my first. I could not wait for the bar to close at night so that I could drink at my own pace, alone. The nights that turned into mornings became very frequent until eventually the arrival of the pub cleaner became my cue to go to leave the bar. Gerry was distraught and pleaded with me to talk to Dr.

Harkin, but I always refused. I knew that a treatment plan of any kind could only begin with my not drinking and I had no intention of agreeing to that. Life would be too impossible without alcohol.

Alcohol was actually keeping me alive because without it I would, without any doubt, take my own life. It allowed me to distance myself from the pain and helped me to dissociate from me, from the me that I knew to be pathetic, inadequate and grew to despise.

Physically I was becoming very unwell and was losing a lot of weight which was not a great surprise considering my calorie intake came predominantly from drinking. Attempting to sleep without alcohol was pointless. Everyone and everything seemed to trigger a negative reaction which more often than not set off a series of emotions including sadness and shame.

These feelings instigated a sense of panic that always lead to the same flashback, mum rocking Siobhán as I screamed 'Wake her up Mum!'

My immediate response to all that was to drink until initially it became a blur and eventually a blackout.

The decision to get professional help was taken out of my hands when, on one of the many occasions Gerry came down to the bar in the early hours to try to convince me to go to bed. He found me lying on the floor, unconscious. Because he was unable to rouse me, he telephoned for an ambulance. When I came to in King's College A&E, I was totally disorientated. I was aware of having a cannula in the back of my hand which was connected to an intravenous drip hanging from a post over my head, but it took a few minutes for me to relate that to being in hospital. Gerry was slumped in a chair by the bedside. I watched him sleeping for a while and I felt so guilty for what I was putting him through.

The doctor arrived. As if on cue, Gerry woke up. The doctor introduced himself and immediately began to list the health risks associated with my drinking. He finally finished with the statement, 'if you continue to drink this way you will die within a year'. None of what he said impacted me.

In that moment I realised that I did not care if I died.

The doctor was obviously waiting for a response from me, but it was Gerry who spoke.

"What can we do doctor?" he asked.

"She needs to stop drinking!" That sentence hung in the air as Gerry looked at me, heartbroken yet hopeful. Without saying a word, he was begging me to agree. I could not answer him.

After a few days of treatment, I was in a much better frame of mind. Gerry and I spoke a lot about our future, and we agreed that it would be easier for me to stay off the drink if I was not in the Tankard. Everything and everyone there held a memory of Siobhán. It was her only home, and everything associated with the place was a constant reminder that she was no longer there. So, we decided to contact the brewery and ask for a quieter pub outside of the city.

Our area manager was very compassionate when we told him about our decision. Of course, we did not mention anything about my drinking.

When I was discharged from hospital I did not return to the Tankard. Instead, I stayed with Gerry's sister Joanne until the arrangements were made for us to move to another pub. Joanne and Roy were fantastic and for the time that I was there I did not drink. The doctor from King's College put me on a cocktail of medications which helped with my appetite and my inability to sleep. He also prescribed an antidepressant which lifted my mood and I noticed that there were times 'when I thought that life could be manageable without alcohol.

Within a month we had moved to The Queen's Arms in Kent. Everything went well for a while but for no apparent reason, the inevitable happened and I started drinking again. Initially, I was motivated to stay sober for Gerry's sake but the reality of having to live with all the pain became too much.

At first, Gerry was really angry, and he was certainly entitled to be. What was to be our new start had become the old nightmare. Before long, my drinking behaviour became a repeat of what it had been. We both realised that the idea of moving in the hope that a change of venue would cure me was a futile dream.

I felt terrible that I had let Gerry down. He would never have moved out of the city except that he believed it would be better for me. He found the publican's life in the country too quiet and thrived on the buzz of the city, so we decided to move back.

"Arl, this has to be the last time" he warned.

"I can't deal with it anymore. You are killing yourself and I can't stand by and watch you do it. You have to promise to stop drinking. Get whatever help you need but please stop".

"This time I'll do it Gerry, I promise. I'll go back to the doctor and get back on the medication. I'll do whatever I need to do to stay sober. I promise".

I meant every word. I was adamant that I would stay off the drink.

I have no idea what cock and bull story Gerry gave to the brewery but whatever it was, we somehow not only managed to stay employed but were offered a well-established pub with a good reputation called the King's Head in Wandsworth, a small borough south west of the city. I knew that staying sober while working in the pub trade was not going to be easy, but I was determined to do it. For the next 6 months I stuck to the regimen of medication and *stayed on the wagon*. Gerry stopped watching what I was pouring into my glass and we both finally started to believe that we were going to make it through the most horrific time that any couple would have to endure.

Our usual Tuesday night out had fallen by the wayside somewhere along the line, but we had recently resumed it. On one such Tuesday, while sitting in a Greek restaurant in Putney, Gerry handed me a small, gift wrapped box. It was a long time ago when I had stopped trying to figure out what anniversary or important date I might have forgotten and discovered that Gerry was just a romantic who did not need a special occasion to do something special. Like a child on Christmas morning, I eagerly ripped off the paper to open the box. Inside lay a key, a car key! I was overwhelmed and started to cry.

"Hey, what's the matter? I thought you'd be chuffed. I got Joanne's bloke to get it. Roy knows his cars so it's not a lemon".

Gerry had no interest in cars and had never even learned how to drive. I had passed my driving test when we were in the Tarmon but I never had my own car. I am sure the reason that we never got around to buying a car was due to my drinking.

"Of course I'm chuffed though I don't know what make and model it is yet. Gerry, this means that you trust me now, not to drink I mean".

"Yeah. You've done brilliant Arl. I think that we are

going to be ok".

"I love you so much", I said.

"Sure, why wouldn't you?", he asked.

The car was a red 1970 Austin Morris 1100 and I absolutely loved it. We called it 'Betsy'. It had only one owner from new and it was immaculate, inside and out. From the first time I drove it, I was instantly confident. Learning to drive up around King's Cross prepared me well for city traffic and I had no fear weaving in and out between the lanes, just like every other driver trying to get from A to B as quickly as possible. Every now and again Gerry and I would pick a place on the map and just take a day off to drive there. We went to Oxford, Portsmouth and Brighton to name just a few. I loved driving and took every opportunity that presented itself, to get behind the wheel.

On nights in the pub, when a regular customer might have had one too many and there was a long wait for a local cab, I would offer to drive them home. I only ever volunteered to do this when the customer was a woman or if it was a couple. Most times my offer was gratefully accepted. From this came the idea to start my own cab firm. However, I had no intention of becoming a cab driver myself. My plan was to have as many drivers as possible, with me running the office until I was in a position to hire staff.

Gerry, as always supported me 100%, even though it would mean that he would have to take on a part-time bar person to help cover my shifts. We did not know how the brewery would feel about my *moonlighting,* but Gerry reckoned that as long as there was no drop in the takings, they would have no reason to question anything. In fact, Gerry and I believed that having the cab firm could only boost custom which would mean that the increase in the takings would cover the cost of extra staff and much more.

The mini-cab business was very straight forward and took little organisation to set up. The company was called Cara Cars, and as the owner, it was my job to drum-up business for the drivers who came to me for work. Being a landlady was a huge advantage because most of the pubs in the locality agreed to support us by using our firm. Every driver was self-employed and responsible for the legalities concerning their vehicles and themselves. Each car was fitted with a cab radio, which the driver rented from the company on a monthly basis. Having the radios meant that a driver seldom had to come to the office as they were given the jobs while on the road.

Initially I manned the office until the company was financially able to pay an office controller. This meant that I was working long hours, often into the early hours of the next morning. The company expanded as we secured contracts from a variety of businesses delivering parcels as well as people across the city, day and night. Being a cab controller was not an easy job. It involved a great deal of timing and planning, to have a driver at the right location within a promised timeframe and to make it cost effective for everyone involved.

Very often, I worked 24 hours straight and sometimes even more. I had a makeshift bed in the office in order to grab a few hours sleep when the phones were silent for brief periods. Gerry was not at all happy about this, but I explained that it would only be this way until the business could afford to pay staff. I was not entirely happy about the situation myself because although the office was very safe and secure it was lonely when the other offices in the block closed for the night.

Gerry soon rectified that. One evening he arrived at the office with a dog on a lead. It was a west highland terrier and at first glance it looked so funny for such a big man to have such a small dog.

"Aw where did you get him?" I asked as I bent down to stroke the dog's head.

"It's not a him, it's a her", he corrected me.

"Ok. Where did you get her?"

"From a bloke in the pub".

I continued to stroke the dog and waited for him to say more.

"The dog belonged to this bloke's wife. She passed away recently and he is moving into a smaller place. He can't take the dog with him so he's looking for a good home. I thought she'd be great company for you. What do you think?"

In the length of time that it took him to say this I had fallen in love with the dog.

"What's her name?" I asked

"Sasha but you could change that if you wanted".

"No, Sasha is perfect. No point in confusing her. A new home will be enough for her to deal with without a new name too".

"So, we're keeping her then?" he asked although he already knew the answer.

"Gerry, she's gorgeous. Of course, we're keeping her". I affirmed.

From that moment on Sasha and I became inseparable. Everywhere I went, she went too. I never used the lead with her because she never left my side, even when we were out walking. She loved being in the car and stood up in the front passenger seat looking out the window, hail, rain or shine. She was very protective of me and growled when anyone came too close, even Gerry.

Very quickly, I could not imagine my life without her, and I worried about the day when I would lose her. I would instantly fall into a panic and become hugely anxious just thinking about it. At these times it was as though she could read my thoughts, because she would jump up on my lap in, what I believed, was an effort to reassure me.

Within a few months Cara Cars was doing well enough financially to take on a part-time office controller. However, I was still covering a lot of the over-night shifts especially at the weekends. It was not unusual for me to work from Friday evening to Monday morning, only returning to the pub for a shower and a change of clothes. Although I enjoyed having my own business the long hours were taking their toll. My sleep pattern became very erratic and I was struggling to sleep even when I was not working. I felt tired all the time and I was terrified that I would have to give up the business if I did not do something.

My first thought was that I could have a few drinks on my night off. Alcohol always helped me to sleep and if I only drank once a week everything would be fine. My second thought was my promise to Gerry, so I did not entertain the first one for long.

One evening, when there were a few drivers in the cab office, I brought up the subject. Many drivers, who worked long hours, had the same sleep problems that I had, and their solution was very simple and very effective, cannabis.

Some of the effects of smoking a joint are that it makes a person feel relaxed and sleepy, so I thought that I would give it a try. And it worked.

Initially, I only used it when I could not sleep but I discovered that it had other benefits. I found that because it gave me a sense of slowing things down, I was feeling less anxious. Since losing Siobhán, I had become even more tense and fearful at random times while at other times I felt detached and numb. Smoking cannabis helped to level things out.

Very quickly, I was using it a few times a week, sometimes more and this meant that I was often lethargic and unmotivated at work. In an attempt to counteract this, I began using cocaine. The stimulant effect of cocaine made me feel more alert and energetic and I liked it. I liked the idea of being able to control my emotions. With the use of a drug I could choose to feel *up or down*.

Of course, I knew that this meant that I was stifling any real emotions I had, and this was having a detrimental effect on my relationship with Gerry. He had no idea about my drug use, and I allowed him to believe that my erratic behaviour was as a result of the grief of losing Siobhán. In a way it was but deep inside I knew I was being disingenuous with him. Yet, I did not want to stop using cannabis or cocaine. In a way that I found too difficult to explain, even to myself, I felt the need to just use something.

I could not face reality on my own.

The only way that I believed I could survive was with the aid of something outside of myself, and I thought that had to be either alcohol or drugs. I knew this way of thinking was dysfunctional and in moments of clarity I could see the harm I was doing. This was not the way I wanted to spend the rest of my life.

In time the cab business and the pub business were both doing well and with that came less pressure for Gerry and myself. My drug use lessened along with my work hours and I had decided that I would stop using drugs completely.

I was not yet 25 years old and I felt that I owed it to myself and to Gerry to at least try to look to the future. They say that losing a child can often destroy a couples' relationship but for some the shared pain can bring them closer together. Sometimes I found it difficult to know which scenario applied to us.

Although we were engaged neither of us were in any hurry to get married or to have another child. We felt that we needed time to accept that Siobhán was gone before we embarked on any new plans.

We were both content enough to continue as we were with the businesses and decided to do whatever we needed to strengthen our relationship for the future.

Chapter 9

One Saturday night Gerry and I arranged to meet up with Joanne and Roy in a pub in Shepherd's Bush, an area in West London that is very popular with the Irish community. Because I was not drinking Gerry and I travelled from Wandsworth in Betsy and Roy was delighted to see that the car he had advised Gerry to buy was running so well. As last orders were being called in the bar, we decided to go the late-night kebab shop on Shepherd's Bush Green for something to eat. When we got there every table was occupied but we happily chatted away as we waited our turn in the queue to be seated.

Suddenly, over the noise of the busy restaurant I heard a laugh that sent shivers all over my body. I recognised the distinctive loud guffaw of the man who had abused me when I was 7 years old. I was instantly transported back in time and became the terrified child who was being abused. All of the coping mechanisms that I had developed and perfected over the years became useless as I froze in terror to the spot that I was standing on.

I became aware that Gerry realised that something was wrong when he looked anxiously into my face. His lips were moving but I could not hear what he was saying. The only sound I heard was that laugh. I felt Gerry put his arm around me and steer me out of the restaurant. As soon as the outside air hit me, my stomach turned over and I threw up on the pavement. This purging brought me back to the present and although I could now hear Gerry asking me what was wrong, somehow, I felt that I could not tell him the truth.

"It was just so stuffy in there. I felt queasy", I replied.

"You went as white as a sheet. I thought you were going to faint", Gerry said.

By now Joanne and Roy were also outside, concerned about what was going on.

"I'm fine really". I tried to convince myself as much as them. "I just want to go home".

"OK but you're not driving. We'll get a cab", Gerry declared.

"I can't leave the car here all night. It'll be towed before we get back to pick it up tomorrow. I'm ok honestly. I just want to get out of here".

After some toing and froing from everyone about what was the best thing to do, we were all finally inside the car and on our way to drop Joanne and Roy back to their flat in Chiswick. We left them with promises to go in the next time that we were out together and within a couple of minutes Gerry and I were on our way home to Wandsworth. I drove in silence as I put all of my energy into concentrating on getting us there in one piece. At that time of night, the traffic was very light, and we arrived at the King's Head in about half an hour.

As soon as we got upstairs Gerry asked, "What's going on?"

"Gerry can we talk about it tomorrow. I don't think I can discuss it right now".

"Well now I'm even more worried Arl. What the hell happened back there?"

I knew that it would not be fair to leave him worrying all night, so I told him.

"The guy who first abused me was in the restaurant".

"Why didn't you tell me? I'd have beat the pervert to a pulp", Gerry shouted.

"Maybe that's why I didn't tell you!", I yelled back at

him.

"You would have been arrested if you touched him".

"I wouldn't have cared if I got arrested!" he roared.

"I'd have feckin' killed the bastard". Gerry was pacing around punching the fist of one hand into the palm of the other.

Suddenly we both realised that Sasha was barking her head off. She was obviously scared and confused about all the shouting. I lifted her up to me to soothe her and she began to settle down. I continued to hold her as I sat down on the sofa.

Gerry had calmed down too and when he came to sit beside me Sasha growled at him warningly. She had a lot of attitude for a small dog. We both laughed at her constant determination to protect me and I hugged her closer as I asked quietly "what do we do now?"

Gerry's instant response was, "We have to go the Police".

"I don't know if I can do that. It's going to open up a *can of worms* and I'm not sure that I can handle that".

"Arl, you have to!", Gerry insisted.

"Once a pervert, always a pervert! He is probably still abusing children. You have to report him!"

"I'm not just thinking about me. This is going to affect my whole family. And you too. The Police will want to talk to everyone, won't they?"

"I never thought of that, but you still have to do it".

"Maybe it wasn't him. I can't really say that I recognised him from his laugh, can I? They'll think I'm crazy".

I knew that I was just looking for a way out because I had absolutely no doubt about who he was. For years that laugh reverberated around inside my head. It was unmistakable and unforgettable.

"Let's sleep on it", Gerry suggested. "We can talk about it tomorrow".

I lay awake all night, petrified. I knew that the threat the abuser held over me when I was a child could no longer hurt me or anyone else yet the idea of telling terrified me beyond reason. I became the little child again who was afraid of something awful happening if I told. But what Gerry said was true, I had to tell to stop him from hurting other children.

Finally dawn came and I got up to go to the kitchen to make coffee. Gerry was only a few minutes behind me.

"You alright?" he asked.

"Sorry dumb question".

"Gerry, I think you are right. I do have to tell the Police. But I can't say that I know this guy is child abuser just because of his laugh".

"What do we do then?"

"It came to me last night when I was lying awake in the dark. Let's look up the electoral register. I know his name and the name of the small village he comes from in Ireland. There could not be two men of the same age, with the same name in a small village. Thing is though we'd have to find out how to get hold of the electoral register".

"That's easy", Gerry said.

"Anyone can ask to see the register in the local library. I'll pretend I'm him if they start asking questions".

This was becoming very real and I could feel myself starting to panic. Gerry could obviously sense my fear and tried to reassure me.

"We'll take it one step at a time. Let's just check the register and then take it from there ok?" I nodded my head in agreement, but I could feel the anxiety coursing through every nerve in my body.

Being a Sunday, it was easy to arrange for extra staff to cover our shifts at work. No one minded working on a Sunday because the hours were less but the pay was the same. We set off even before the pub opened. I felt that I would not be able to take on the added pressure of driving, so we took a cab to Hammersmith. Shepherds Bush comes under the London borough of Hammersmith & Fulham so we thought that the main library in Hammersmith would probably be our best bet to get access to the register.

The smaller local libraries would not have been open on a Sunday, but the bigger ones always opened for a couple of hours on a Sunday morning so that people could go in to read the national newspapers.

As we walked towards the big old building, I became aware that I was following Gerry as if I was in a trance. He took the lead and I just followed. When we got to the reception desk in the library, I heard him ask the woman behind the desk if he could see the register and within a couple of minutes, we were sitting at a table with the register in front of us. He found the name we were looking for and wrote down the address that went with it. There was no one else with the same name on the register. He returned the register to the receptionist and we walked out.

When we stepped outside, I exhaled loudly and only then realised that I had been holding my breath.

"Well?" Gerry looked at me questioningly.

He was looking over my shoulder and when I turned to see what he indicating to I saw the all too familiar blue light that is traditionally found at the entrance to every police station.

"Not yet", I pleaded. "We have to be sure it's him".

"How are we going to be able to do that?" he asked.

"Can we go to the address? We might see him".

"We can't just knock on the door and ask for him!" I could hear that he was getting frustrated.

"Can't we just go there first, please?" I begged him.

"Ok. We'll get an A to Z and see where the place is".

The A to Z is the London street map which can be purchased in almost every tube and train station as well as in most confectionary and newspaper shops in the city. We had the option of going back into the library to look up the address but decided against it, just in case we were pushing our luck. Instead we walked to the tube station where we could have a coffee and a sit down as we studied the map. Gerry found the road we were looking for almost immediately and we noticed that it was within walking distance from the station.

"Let's not hang about", Gerry said.

"Get it over with as soon as possible".

"What are we going to do when we get there?" I asked.

"Let's get there first and then decide", he answered.

"You have to promise not to *lose it* if we do see him. Otherwise, I'm not going".

He agreed.

It took only a few minutes to walk to the road we were looking for and just a few more to find the right door number. There was a van parked outside the house with the name of a construction company written on the side. I was more convinced than ever that this was the man who had abused me as it appeared that he had even stayed in the same line of work. It was a strange feeling standing outside the house. Knowing that he could literally be only a few yards away sent tremors all over me. In my mind's eye I could see his face.

171

Over the years I had tried to eradicate the image but no matter how hard I tried it never left me.

Gerry's voice broke into my thoughts.

"Look, there's a pub. We can watch the house from there if we sit outside. It's a cul de sac so if anyone comes out, they have to pass that way".

"He could be in the pub!" I said in near panic.

Gerry took my hand and we walked into the pub together. Sunday mornings were usually quiet in the small backstreet pubs, so it did not take long for me to realise that he was not in there. We got our drinks and went outside to begin our surveillance.

While we were sitting there the minutes seemed to drag by. We finished our first drink and decided to have another. Gerry was having his usual pint of cider and I had a coffee. I was feeling very jittery and the coffee probably did not help. I would have loved a glass of wine, or anything alcoholic but I knew that that would have not ended well. I had been sober since Gerry and I took over the King's Head and I was quite proud of that.

Gerry suddenly said, "someone's coming out of the house".

He said it very quietly, almost a whisper, but it sounded like a roar inside my head. My anxiety went into overdrive. A man and a woman exited the front door of the house and started walking towards us. I tried not to look but I could not pull my eyes away as I fixated on the face of the man. My heart rate went up with every step he took.

As he came nearer it struck me that he was not as big as I remembered. It reminded me of the day that I took Shauna, my niece to school in the Little Angels. Returning to my old primary school as an adult felt very strange because everything there seemed so small in comparison to how I experienced it as a child.

The couple were about to enter the pub when the man stopped and looked directly at me. He must have sensed that I was watching him intently. For a brief second, time stood still as I held his gaze. Then he turned and followed the woman into the pub.

"Well?" Gerry began.

In a voice that did not sound like mine, I responded with two simple words, "it's him".

I got up from the table we were sitting at and started to walk away. Gerry quickly followed. Without thinking I walked towards Hammersmith Broadway, the big shopping centre that provides access to the underground station. I felt strangely calm, but I also felt the need to get away.

I sat down on the first public seating bench that was vacant inside the Broadway. Gerry sat down beside me and waited for me to speak.

Finally, I said, "it's definitely him".

"Are you certain sure?" Gerry asked.

"No doubt about it", I replied. "I saw that face every day for 3 years. It's definitely him".

Gerry put his arm around me and asked, "what do you want to do now?".

"I want to get out of here", I said.

"I don't think I can cope with anything more today. I suddenly feel absolutely shattered".

We walked back out to the entrance of the shopping centre and Gerry hailed a cab to bring us back to Wandsworth. When we arrived at the King's Head, I went straight upstairs to our private living area. As I threw myself down on the sofa in the sitting room my mind was in turmoil. I was struggling to put a name on exactly what I was feeling. The contradictory sensations going on in my body did nothing to help. My skin was tingling as I shivered with the cold and within minutes I was breaking out in a hot sweat. My stomach turned over as though I would vomit but there was only painful dry retching after I raced to the bathroom. My whole body felt extremely tired, but I could not sit still.

I could hear Gerry making tea in the kitchen.

He arrived in the sitting room holding a mug of piping hot tea. Handing it to me he said, "I put 2 sugars in it. That's supposed to be good for shock, so they say".

I never took sugar, either in tea or coffee but the hot sweet liquid did seem to settle things down. We sat in silence for what seemed like a very long time and when I had finished the tea, I was certainly feeling a lot calmer.

I worked the shift behind the bar that evening in autopilot. Being able to disassociate from my thoughts and feelings allowed me to perform as normal, a skill that I learned to depend on over the years. However, it seemed to work best when I was intent on carrying out some kind of task. It failed me later that night when I was lying awake in bed thinking about what I was going to do next. I knew that if I went to the police to report the abuse that things were going to change for a lot of people. I thought about how it would affect Mum and the rest of my family, because they would all have to go through a police interview.

My family never had any involvement with the police, and I knew that they would find it very daunting to be part of an investigation. They might think that there was no sense in bringing it up after all this time, and it was better to just let it go. I even thought about *his* Mum, and his wife and his children and grandchildren, if he had any. Thinking about the possibility of him having access to children helped me to decide.

Into the darkness I said, "I'm going to talk to the police".

I knew that Gerry was lying awake too. "I'll be with you every step of the way", the darkness replied.

By the time morning came I knew what I wanted to do. I was not going to make an official report. I would simply make the police aware of a man living in the area who was a danger to children. I would give them his name and address and inform them that should a complaint be made against him that they should investigate it thoroughly. In this way I felt content that I had done the right thing while still safeguarding myself and my family.

Once I had made my decision, I did not want to delay so Gerry and I travelled back to Hammersmith that afternoon when the pub closed. On the journey I rehearsed exactly what I was going to say and vowed that I would say no more and no less.

When we got to Hammersmith Police Station, I did not hesitate. I walked up the steps, took a deep breath and pushed open the main door to go in. There was an officer sitting at a desk, behind a Perspex screen who looked up when we went in. As there was no one waiting, Gerry and I walked straight over to him.

"Could we speak to someone in private?" Gerry enquired.

"What's it in relation to sir?" the officer asked.

Gerry looked at me, but I had not rehearsed this bit, so I said nothing.

"My fiancée wants to speak with a female officer about something that happened when she was a child".

Gerry looked at me as if to ask if that was ok and I

nodded a 'yes'.

The officer behind the desk instructed us to take a seat while he spoke to someone on the phone. Almost immediately a door to our right opened and a female officer invited us to follow her inside. She led the way to, what was obviously an interview room, and asked Gerry and I to sit down at a table. She sat on the opposite us. Before she said anything further, I spoke. Without drawing a breath, I said exactly what I had rehearsed and memorised.

"I have the name and address of a man who I know is a danger to children. What you do with that information is up to you, but that's all I have to say". I then gave her the name and the address of the man.

With that I got up to leave.

In hindsight it was naïve of me to think that I could make a statement like that to the police and not expect them to want to question me about it. The first thing the officer did was to ask me my name, but I told her that I was uncomfortable to do that. Before I knew what was happening, I was being quizzed about how I knew this man and how I knew that he was a danger to children. Eventually, I told her that he had abused me when I was child but that I did not want to make an official statement about out.

I am not entirely sure what happened after that, but that day was the beginning of a series of events that I had absolutely no control over. Within days I received a phone call from the Guards in Ireland asking me to go home to talk to them about a statement I had made to the police in London. I was stunned and asked why I needed to do that. They informed me that the police in Hammersmith had passed on the information I had given them to the Guards because the 'alleged crime' happened in Ballyshannon and that was where it was going to be investigated.

For the next 6 months or more I felt like I was living in a blur. Gerry and I went home, and I made a statement to the Guards. Gerry also had to make one. Following that my Mum and my family gave statements. The family doctor and my school teachers, including my friend Sr.Sheila were questioned about my unusual behaviour as a child as well as about things that I had said at the time.

Gerry and I tried our best to get on with things in London and some days it was possible to forget that the whole thing was actually going on. When I did think about it, I was angry and upset that things had been taken completely out of my hands. I felt hoodwinked into doing something that I did not want to do and any power that I may have had was taken away from me.

One of the two Guards conducting the investigation rang one day to tell us that the man I had accused of sexually abusing me was finally going to be interviewed. The outcome of that was that he admitted to knowing me and my family as well as to all the time he had spent around our home, but he denied that he had ever sexually abused me.

The next phone call that we received from the Guards was to tell us that they were not taking the investigation any further. They said that regardless of all the statements that my family and other people had given, it came down to my word against his. Without further evidence they were not going to proceed. I was devastated. Although, initially I did not want an official investigation I had no other choice but to accept it when the decision was taken away from me, and now everything that we had gone through was for nothing. He was going to get away with it.

I had always found it very difficult to accept that I was

abused by so many people and over the years I had learned to manage that by blaming him, my first abuser for everything. Whether he knew all of the other abusers or not did not matter to me, but I believed that it was he who made me a victim. Since the police investigation began, I had come to believe that if he was held accountable then I would free me from them all. But that was not going to happen now. I felt that I would have to live the rest of my life as a victim, trapped by my past and in the power of all of those who had abused me. Any hope of being able to live in some sort of normality was gone.

In the months that followed Gerry continued to run the pub and me the cab office. The cab drivers had started complaining about how slow the work was. Previously we had contracts with some of the major businesses that peppered the whole of the A4, the main road from the city to Heathrow Airport, but when the 1990 recession hit Britain, a lot of the big companies closed. Obviously, this meant that all the guaranteed work that we had been getting in the past, was now gone. One by one, the drivers left and very quickly, the business got into trouble. I was struggling every month to pay the bills and although Gerry bailed me out a couple of times by helping to cover some of the costs, eventually I had to close the cab firm.

I did not want to go back into the pub business, so I decided to apply to join the police. I thought that if I became part of the system that I felt had let me down I might be able to help other abuse survivors who were going through the process of an investigation. Once I was accepted for training, I gave it my all. I changed my eating habits and became super fit. I had not told my family that I had applied for the police in case I did not get the job so when I passed all the fitness tests and the final interview, I decided to travel home to tell them.

I had planned on staying in Ireland for only a few days, so I rented a car at Dublin airport. The sun was shining and the drive to Donegal was very pleasant. When I arrived in Ballyshannon, I felt proud to tell Mum and my family about my new job. They were all delighted to see that I was doing something so worthwhile and that I was signing up for a stable and secure career. They were even happier to learn that I was doing ok and that I appeared to be getting on with my life.

My short trip was soon over and all too quickly I was on my way back to Dublin. The weather had changed and by the time I got as far as Cavan it was raining heavily. On the Dublin side of Cavan town, I lost control of the car and hit an empty trailer being towed by an oncoming tractor. Thankfully the driver of the tractor was not hurt but I was seriously injured. My car rolled twice and landed on its roof in a field. The right side of my body was broken and bruised but the most serious injury I sustained was a brain injury. As a result of this I developed epilepsy which meant that I was no longer fit to do the job of a police officer.

I spent about 3 months recuperating and during that time family and friends visited. They all tried to encourage me by suggesting that there were lots of other jobs that I would still be able to do and although I agreed for peace sake, I felt that I had nothing left to invest in another attempt at anything. The brain injury left me with a lot of health issues, including severe headaches, short-term memory loss and an inability to concentrate for any length of time. As well as that I was no longer allowed to drive because as a result of the epilepsy, I was having frequent grand mal seizures. But it was the injury to my spirit that caused the most damage.

As soon as the doctors gave me the all clear to fly, I

returned to London.

Gerry, as always, did his best to be supportive but nothing could remove the overwhelming sensation of hopelessness that now encased me. When I looked back at my life, all I could see was pain and loss, added to that was a despairing sense of injustice. I was so tired of trying to survive, of trying to recover and move on, just to be hit with another life-changing blow. I did not have the strength or the motivation to try again. For me, the usual expectations of a chance at a normal life were over.

It was not fair of me to consider a future with Gerry when I believed that the future held nothing for me. For a while I tried to pretend that I could change how I felt but deep down I knew it was pointless. Gerry knew that I had given up and although he continually tried to reignite some hope in me, he finally realised that nothing could change my views around the futility of continuing to believe that I could ever feel fulfilled or be truly happy in life.

He was very keen for us to have another baby, believing that this would make things better, but I knew in my heart that I would never be able to go through it again. The fear of history repeating itself prevented me from even considering the possibility of having another child. My heart broke for Gerry because I knew that he did not feel the same way. He loved being a Dad and he wanted to have more children, but I knew that it would not happen if he was with me. It would be so unfair of me to continue in the relationship knowing that I would never change my mind, so I had to tell him that it was over.

It was one of the hardest things I ever had to do. Gerry was one of the most important people in my life and I knew that he felt the same way about me. We had shared so much that we both believed that it would be impossible for us not to always be a part of each other's lives. No one else could ever share our joint love and loss of Siobhán and because of that we would always be together in some way.

On the morning I moved out I was heartbroken and although I was tempted to stay, I knew that it would be the wrong thing to do, both for Gerry and for me. I still loved Gerry in my own way, but I knew that it was not the right kind of love for a long-lasting intimate relationship. Gerry merited so much more than I was able to give, and I knew that one day he would meet someone who could give him all the things he so deserved.

With Sasha beside me in the back seat of a cab and a couple of suitcases in the boot we made our way to the flat I had rented in Acton, a few days before.

I now had no source of income and the cost of the rent for the flat was going to be a struggle while I was on disability benefits. Trisha who was a friend I met through the cab business had a house in Hounslow, which is only about 15 minutes from Heathrow Airport, said that I could rent a room from her for half the cost of what I was currently paying and having Sasha with me was no problem so the decision to move from Acton to Hounslow was not a difficult one. Trisha was a teacher at the local comprehensive school and had been living alone since the breakdown of her marriage almost 2 years previously.

She had regularly used the cab firm, so she had met Sasha on a number of occasions. She loved dogs but because she was out of the house for the most part of every day she had decided against getting one, so having Sasha turned out to be a positive rather than a negative which is often the case when trying to find accommodation.

It did not take long for the recession to hit the pub trade and the breweries were closing some of the smaller pubs that were struggling financially. It was decided that the King's Head was one of the pubs to close. Thankfully, they had a management position for Gerry, but it was in Peckham, in South London which was more than an hour away which meant that we would not see one another as often as we used to. For the first time in a long time I felt that I was on my own.

I never contemplated moving back home, even though I knew that a loving and supportive family waited for me there. In my limited worldview at the time I believed that the worst things that had ever happened to me happened there while at the same time much of the best things in my life also happened there, but I found these two perceptions difficult to accurately evaluate.

It was less complicated for me to just stay in London.

Chapter 10

Living day by day was not easy but having Sasha made it much more tolerable. She gave me a reason to get up every day because it was my responsibility to look after her. There were many times when I did not want to get out of bed, to face another day of nothingness, but I had to because I had to bring her outside for her morning *toilet*. Having a dog in London is different to having a dog in Donegal. When I was a child, we always had a dog and when it wanted to go to the loo all we had to do was open the back door to let it out into the field.

In London, having Sasha meant that I had to get dressed and walk her to the park or nearest green area whenever she needed to relieve herself. This simple act, though immensely important to her was even more significant for me because it became a way of survival. Without it, without her I may only have ventured out on a Friday, the day that I had to go to the post office to collect my disability payments.

I met many people in the park, some walking their dogs and some not. Interactions that began with a polite 'good morning' or 'good evening' often emerged over time into more in-depth conversations about what was going on in our lives. It was during one of these times that I met Donna and her Doberman called King. When I saw the Doberman, I was instantly afraid for Sasha. A big dog like that *could have her for breakfast* but when I looked around to pick her up, I saw her chasing the Doberman around the park! The Doberman ran straight to its owner with Sasha hot on his heels.

"Some attack dog eh?", she said with a big smile on her face as the Doberman collided with her nearly knocking her over.

"My name's Donna and this big wuss is King".

"Arylene, and this Westie, who thinks she's an Irish Wolfhound, is Sasha".

Donna was a tattoo artist who owned her own shop in Isleworth and every piece of visible skin, other than on her face, was tattooed.

"You look amazing", I told her.

"Not everyone likes the look", she responded. "But each to their own eh?"

"I have a few myself, and I always planned to have more".

My first tattoo was done by George Bone, a well-known tattoo artist in London at the time. It was a memorial piece for Siobhán and I cherished it.

"Come into the shop. I might have something you'd like", she suggested.

"Money is tight at the minute, but I'd love to pop in just to have a look at the designs".

"No worries. See you later then", and with that she was gone.

That afternoon Sasha and I arrived at the tattoo shop. As I was tying Sasha's lead to the post outside Donna opened the door.

"Bring her in", she said.

"I don't mind well-behaved dogs being in the shop, just so long as they don't venture near the tattooing studio downstairs".

Every inch of wall space in the shop was covered in *flash,* the standard designs found in every tattoo shop.

"Do you have a book of your own stuff?" I asked.

Even though I only had a few tattoos I preferred ones that were more unique to me. Most artists had a book of their own designs which were examples of their custom work. As I was looking through the pages Donna said,

"Are you in a hurry to get away or would you be able to cover the shop for a couple of hours?"

"No, I'm in no rush but what do you want me to do if someone comes in?" I said in a bit of a panic.

"Just ask them to come back after 3pm. I'll just be downstairs tattooing. This guy has been booked in for ages, and I don't want to let him down at the last minute if I can help it. I'll be finished about 3ish. Gary, who usually works here is off sick and I had no time to get cover. You'd be doing me a big favour. I'd have to lock the door if you couldn't do it."

"No worries. Sasha and I will be fine. I can't wait to look through all the tattoo magazines you have here".

Just then the door opened and in walked Donna's pre-booked customer.

She led him to the tattoo studio downstairs and within minutes I could hear the tranquil music that Donna had put on. I could also smell the incense sticks she started burning. All of this added to the calming vibe that lingered around the whole place.

During the time Donna was busy tattooing, a number of people came into the shop just to browse. Some had questions that I was unable to answer for example how long it would take to tattoo a particular design. Others wanted to know about prices and available appointment times but, they were all very content to either return to the shop later or to ring to speak with someone else at another time.

It was not until Donna and her customer appeared at the top of the stairs that I realised that the two hours were up. The time flew by.

"Well, how did you manage?" she asked when her customer had paid and left.

"No problem", I replied.

"There were a few potential customers in but when I explained the situation, they were quite happy to get back to you again".

"Brilliant! Now let me pay you for your time", she said.

"No, it's ok", I said.

"I was doing nothing else and it passed a couple of hours for me".

"Have a tattoo, free of charge", she insisted.

"I won't say 'no' to that. I've been thinking about getting another one but there's no way I could afford it being on benefits".

"Then it's settled. Let's work out what design you like, and we can do it when the shop closes this evening, if that suits you?"

"Yeah, suits me fine", I said eagerly.

"In the meantime, I'd better take Sasha out the back for a wee. She's been looking to go but I didn't want to leave the shop unattended".

As soon as Sasha and I returned to the shop Donna said, "I've had an idea. How would you like to work a couple of days a week for me? You'd be working with Gary most of time so you wouldn't be on your own a lot. What do you say?"

"I can't. Thanks for the offer though", I replied.

"Why not?" she persisted.

"I can't leave Sasha on her own all day and it would be a pain to sort out with the social welfare because I'm on disability".

"You can bring Sasha to work with you and I'll pay you

186

cash in hand. You'll also get staff discount for any tattoos and piercings you want".

I had not bothered to even think about trying to get a job because I still had a lot of problems with headaches and concentration. However, Donna's offer was too good to pass up, so I accepted. I just thought that if it did not work out so be it, I had nothing to lose. But I surprised myself by picking up the run of things very quickly and found that I enjoyed being around the 'tattoo' scene. The type of clientele was very different to what I was used to, and I really liked that. Some of the customers were certainly ordinary people living ordinary lives, but others were what some might consider to be more alternative people living on the fringes of society and it was this group that I was more attracted to.

Within 6 months I had completely changed my appearance. I got more and more tattoos as well as numerous body piercings which made me feel much more comfortable in my own skin. This feeling of ease encouraged me to get more and over the following year I had more facial piercings that most people who were part of the scene.

My appearance also served another very important purpose, it discouraged strangers from talking to me or from even coming near me. I called my new look my *metal mask*. But because of my look people judged me and labelled me a person below their own rank or status. I was not to be trusted and some thought I might even be dangerous. Many times, a person would stand on bus or tube journey when the seat beside me was vacant. At other times a security officer in a shopping mall would follow me from store to store assuming that they were about to catch a thief in the act.

My appearance also got me plenty of other work. I featured in some of the tattoo magazines and this led to my picture being used in other publications for a variety of adverts. I was signed up to an agency called 'Ugly' which provided people with alternative looks as extras for appearances in films and TV shows. But what I found most incredible was that a photograph of me was part of an exhibition in the Tate Modern Art Gallery in London. In all this extrovert behaviour I was being someone else behind my *metal mask*. What people did not know was that I was a damaged and disillusioned person hiding in plain sight.

During this time, I met so many interesting people, and was introduced to the underground club scene of the city. Drugs went hand in hand with the lifestyle that I was now living. A typical week for me was working in the shop Monday and Tuesday, then Wednesday, Thursday or Friday could involve an all-day event as an extra or going to a studio for photographs.

For all of this I would have Sasha with me because as an extra you were hanging around a lot of the time doing nothing and for the short time that I was being filmed or photographed Simone, another extra who also had a dog would keep an eye on her for me. I returned the favour by looking after her dog when she was called. The entire weekend was then spent partying and clubbing.

The only way to maintain this pace was to use drugs. I used cocaine, ecstasy and cannabis every weekend while drinking copious amounts of alcohol at the same time. I thought that I was having the time of my life.

The first indication I had that things were beginning to go wrong was when Trisha asked me to move out of her house in Hounslow. This happened as a result of many episodes of my unacceptable behaviour that was causing her concern. For example, I was mugged at a bus stop on my way home late one night. I was so drunk that I could not give a statement to the police, and because I was not injured, they drove me home. Trisha was not too happy when she was awoken to find police on her doorstep.

On another occasion I was found by the airport police in the early hours of the morning in a field at Heathrow Airport. I had no idea how I got there. I was covered in scratches and bruises, so the police took me to the hospital. I did not have any serious injuries, neither was there any evidence of a sexual assault so I was discharged. Once again, the police brought me home and when I arrived at the house Trisha was waiting for me. The police had contacted her at her school so that she would be there when we arrived.

When the police left Trisha began "Arylene I'm so relieved that you are ok", she said as she held the sitting room door open for me.

I could hear Sasha barking before I saw her but within seconds, she was jumping up for me to lift her.

I sat down on the sofa with Sasha in my lap and Trisha sat beside me. "You have to change what you're doing before you get really hurt or even killed".

"You sound like the police", I responded.

"I'm sorry about the drama but I'm ok".

"I can't sit back and watch you do this to yourself". She paused for a minute and then said, "you'll have to go. Find somewhere else to live".

"Ok", I said simply.

It did not seem strange to me that I was not hurt by her decision to kick me out. I knew that I was distancing myself from the people around me. If they were not close to me then they could not hurt me. I was living behind this *metal mask* all the time now and although I believed that I was protecting myself, I also knew that my fear of trusting people meant that I was always alone.

"You don't have to leave straight away", she told me kindly. "Wait 'til you have something proper sorted out".

"Na it's ok really. I know that having the police coming to the house is not ideal, especially with your job. I've a mate who will put me up for a while. She's an extra as well and she has a dog who gets on really well with Sasha. I'll give her a ring", I said as I lifted the phone to dial Simone's number. Following a five-minute conversation my new living arrangement was organised.

Simone was delighted that Sasha and I were moving in with her and her dog Billy. The situation seemed perfect as we both lived such similar lives. She also insisted that we could stay for as long as we needed rent free. Her father paid her rent to the council every month by direct debit and she had no interest in making any extra money by way of rent.

"You pay the electric and that will do", she said.

"Deal", I responded with delight.

An added bonus was that her flat was in Twickenham which was still only a bus ride for me to get to work in the tattoo shop. However, I was beginning to feel that how I might get to work would not be an issue for much longer. Donna had already spoken to me about her dissatisfaction around my being late again on the previous Monday morning. I told her that I had simply over-slept, but I sensed that she was well aware that it was because I was, yet again hung-over from a weekend of drinking and drugging.

I had been working in the tattoo shop for 2 years and I was beginning to feel quite resentful about it at times. Those times were mostly on a Monday morning when I felt too sick to go in but felt that I had to. So, after another few weeks of trying and often failing in my commitment to Donna I decided to give up the job. She was not at all surprised when I told her, in fact I think she was probably relieved.

Leaving the shop meant leaving a lot of the people that I hung out with. They were friends of Donna's and I was no longer part of that group. I was ok with that because I was tiring of the nightclub scene and often preferred a night in, drinking and smoking dope. In fact, it was much better to be indoors because I could get as drunk and as stoned as I wanted without the worry of how to get home.

It was ideal living with Simone because she felt the same way as I did. She had also outlived the club scene and preferred to have friends' round to the flat rather than to go out. Most nights there would be people there, drinking, drugging and playing music.

Simone and I got on so well together which may have been partly due to her past having been every bit as dysfunctional as mine though for different reasons. We seldom spoke of the specifics, but she voiced her hurts and her losses in the songs that she wrote. She was a fantastic guitar player and sang with passion and pain and we recognised each other as broken people. As kindred spirits we saw ourselves as unconventional outsiders and lived with little or no routine or discipline.

When the agency telephoned with the offer of work, we sometimes took it and sometimes did not, depending on how much money we had. When we were short of cash, we would simply take a tube into the city and find a pitch to busk. With the dogs, Sasha and Billy lying happily at our feet on a rug in a subway, Simone and I would sing while she played in the hope of entertaining the volume of people travelling through the tunnel. Those in a generous frame of mind would throw their loose change in the guitar case lying open in front of us. We would buy alcohol with some of the money we made and sit drinking in the nearest park as Sasha and Billy ran around playing together until they were exhausted and ready to go home for dinner.

It was impossible to pin-point when I realised that I had feelings for Simone. At different stages throughout my life I struggled with my sexuality which I felt was probably not surprising considering I had been abused. When I was a teenager the very thought of being gay horrified me because it highlighted the fact that I was so different when really, I just wanted to be the same as everyone else. For years I never allowed these feelings to surface, but I realised that as I was beginning to discover who I really was, being gay was a part of that. Being sexually abused as a child had stolen my identity and from that time onwards, I felt that I was a nobody, struggling to fit in. I was now realising that not fitting in was ok.

Simone just seemed to know how I felt and I was delighted to know that she had developed feelings for me too. We lived as a couple for over a year until one day a phone call changed everything. Simone's Dad had died suddenly, and she needed to go home to Yorkshire immediately. She had no idea when she would be back.

Left to my own devices it did not take long for my life to spiral further out of control. People still came around at night to party but now they were often there long into the following day. We would just continue to drink and use drugs until we fell unconscious and could do no more.

Every few days I would insist on everyone giving me space to clean up the flat and getting some shopping in. The shopping seldom differed from dog food, a loaf of bread, a block of cheese, cans of beer and whatever wine or cheap spirit was on special offer that week.

Simone rang every day at first then only a few times a week. When I asked her when she might be returning to London, she said that her Mum was not coping well with the sudden loss of her husband and Simone felt that she could not leave her just yet. Although I missed her, I realised that, at times, I had a sense of relief every time she said that she would not be coming back for another while. Her return would undoubtedly change the pattern of drinking I had developed since she left, and I did not want that to happen just yet.

The agency also rang every so often, but I was usually too drunk to go to a job and eventually they stopped ringing all together.

I soon got to the stage where I no longer wanted to have people around me. I refused to open the door when anyone came calling and the old visitors quickly realised that they needed to find another place to party. There were times when I did not want to even talk to Simone and so I did not always answer the phone when I recognised her number on caller ID.

I would sit alone for hours, drinking and ruminating on my past, trying to make sense of everything that had happened. When the memories evoked the searing pain of loss I drank some more. I drank to drown the loss of my childhood, the loss of being a mother, a grandmother and the loss of myself, the person I was supposed to be had I not been a victim of abuse. I drank to numb the painful feelings that I had no control over, to erase the tormenting images inside my head and to ease the hammering in my chest that seemed to erupt out of nowhere.

However, it was becoming more difficult to drink away

the memories that tortured me or to drown out the persistent negative thoughts and feelings that overwhelmed me. As time went on, the more I drank the more ashamed I felt and the more I despised myself. I was a failure with nothing to show for my life and I did not care whether I lived or died. My only comfort was a drink.

I drank to get drunk, and literally to get out of my own head, to get away from myself. Drinking gave me a little bit of free time away from my head, some space away from all the confusion and pain continually rushing around inside me. I had no real friends left and I had very sporadic contact with my family. I was very aware of what I was doing but could not break away from the repetitive behaviour.

Yet in contradiction to this was the fact that I felt that my drinking gave me a sense of control over my life. I believed that I was actually 'deciding' to drink and that I was choosing the life I was living. Everything had been taken away from me at different times in my life and I had no choice or control over that, but drinking allowed me the opportunity to decide, to whether I gave up on life or not. Even that self-destructive way of thinking gave me a feeling of control, while all the time my main objective was to anesthetise feeling, feeling anything at all.

I was awoken out of a stupor one day by a thunderous banging on the front door of the flat. A man's voice shouted through the letterbox, "Bailiff, open up!"

Sasha's incessant barking destroyed any ploy to deny that there was anyone home. When I opened the door 2 men instantly walked into the flat forcing me to take a step backwards. I quickly lifted Sasha out of the way.

"We are here to take possession of this property on behalf of Richmond council", one of them said.

Sasha continued to bark so loudly that I had to put her in another room so that I could hear what was going on.

"What do you mean, 'take possession of'?" I asked.

"The rent is 4 months overdue on this flat, can you pay it? If not, we are here to evict you today."

"Don't you have to give notice? Where am I supposed to go?".

The man's tone softened a little.

"Look love, you got loads of notice. The council have been sending letters for months and getting no reply".

There had been a lot of post for Simone that had been piling up on the worktop in the kitchen. Many of the envelopes had 'final demand' written in red ink across the top but I had just *filed* them with all the rest.

It was only then that I realised just how long Simone had been away. It also struck me that it had been some time since I had heard from her. Obviously, at some stage the direct debit arrangement to pay the rent had been stopped indicating that she had no intention of coming back.

"I've no-where to go", I said again.

"Could you give me a few days to arrange something?"

"Sorry love, you have to leave today", he said.

The other man spoke for the first time saying, "get yourself down to the council and they'll put you in emergency accommodation. Not sure if you can have the dog with you though".

There was no way that I was going anywhere without Sasha. The 2 men stood and watched as I packed my things into one rucksack. It did not take long. I put Sasha's dog food and the last 2 cans of beer out of the fridge into a plastic bag to take with me.

I stood at the bus stop across the road from the flat, my

mind a blank. A bus pulled up and the driver opened the door, waiting for me to get on.

"I'm not going anywhere", I told him.

"Get the hell out of the bus stop then!" he shouted angrily as he drove off.

I thought of Gerry and knew that I could go to him. When the next bus arrived at the stop, Sasha and I got on and started the journey to Peckham.

I was so ashamed to have to arrive on Gerry's doorstep, *cap in hand*, but I knew that I had no-where else to go.

When I told him how I felt he admonished, "don't ever feel that way! You can always come to me, no matter what!" I knew that I did not deserve his kindness, but I was so grateful to have him. I really had no one else to turn to.

The pub in Peckham was brewery owned so it was not possible for Sasha and me to stay for more than a couple of days. Gerry said that he would make a few calls and arrange an appointment with the housing officer at Southwark Council to get me a more permanent place.

"I got to know a few people from Labour HQ when we were in the Tankard," he said.

"Someone might be able to do us a favour and get you bumped up to the top of the housing list". Gerry always managed to get to know the *right* people wherever he went because he always reckoned 'you would never know when you might need them'.

When we got to the council offices a man led us into a small room and invited us to sit down. After a lot of form filling and very little discussion the man handed me a set of keys to a flat in the Elephant & Castle and said, "go have a look. If you want it, it's yours".

Within minutes we were out on the street and Gerry was

hailing down a cab to bring us to the address that was written on a piece of cardboard attached to the keys.

"How did you manage that?" I asked him incredulously.

"It's not what you know......" he replied as he smirked and tapped the side of his nose with his forefinger.

The flat was on the 12th floor of a tower block, surrounded by numerous other tower blocks. The place was a maze of tall concrete structures that all look exactly the same. When we finally found the entrance to the block that we were looking for we discovered that the lift was out of order, so we had to use the stairs.

The very distinctive odour of marijuana hung heavily in the air and other drug paraphernalia littered the stair wells. By the time we reached the door number to the flat we were looking for we were both tired out and I had totally lost my bearings.

"If I go out, I'll never find my way back!", I gasped.

Gerry put the key in the lock and had to turn it three times before the door opened.

"There are three bolts in the lock. No one's going to pick that to break in", he explained.

A stifling dead heat hit us the minute we walked into the flat and it was very apparent that no one had lived there for quite some time. We both walked around, opening windows as we went.

"Amazing view", I said sarcastically as I looked out of the sitting room window. I was looking directly into a 12th floor flat on the tower block opposite.

"You needn't take this", Gerry said. "We could probably get another one somewhere else".

"No. I'm fine with this. Actually, I quite like it. Thanks Gerry", I said as I put my arms around him in a tight hug of love and gratitude.

"OK. I'm not too far away if you get any grief. Just give me a bell".

As Sasha and I moved in that evening I thought about how grateful I was to have Gerry in my life. Within a couple days he rang to check on how I was settling in and after that we returned to the level of contact that we previously had with one another. Then, about 6 months later Gerry told me that he was in a new relationship and I knew that our contact would have to be very minimal, if at all. The right thing for me to do was to take a big step back, so that he and his new partner could make a go of it. Whatever happened for me in the future Gerry deserved to have a life free of the baggage that I carried.

I was now in my mid 30's and it was time that I stood on my own two feet.

Chapter 11

Over the next number of years my life spiralled further down the path of self-destruction. My drinking progressed into an act that had no purpose, other than to appease the addiction that I had to alcohol. I continued to use drugs but only as part of a process that enabled me to continue drinking. Stimulants such as cocaine or speed as well as ecstasy kept me awake for days while ensuring that I could drink more and eat less. Using cannabis and different benzodiazepines, such as Valium or Librium meant I could eat and sleep which gave me the energy to start the whole process all over again. This pattern became my way of living, or rather my way of surviving.

However, when money was sparse, my drug use lessened. When it came down to choosing between alcohol or drugs, I always chose alcohol. Outside the madness of addiction, the only thing I cared about was my dog, Sasha. I loved her more than I loved myself. Feeding her was my priority while I sacrificed my own food in order to buy drink. I kept her warm and safe while I risked my own life on a daily basis, just by being an alcoholic and a drug user.

I frequently woke up in a hospital bed, wired up to drips and machines with no idea about where I was or of how I got there. Most times, I was told someone would have phoned for an ambulance because I had a seizure while in a pub, or just that I had been found lying on the street or in a park. It was impossible to tell whether these seizures were as a result of my epilepsy or if they were alcohol or drug induced.

Sometimes I would fall unconscious while sitting at a bus stop or on the bus while I tried to make my way home. In these instances, it would have been the police who picked me up. When I came around and realised that I was in a hospital, I would immediately take out the drips and pull off the stickers on my chest that were attached to the machines, so that I could leave. My aim was firstly to pick up Sasha, usually from the nearest police station or on occasion from Battersea dogs' home and then I would be off to get another drink.

Every waking hour of every day was consumed with thoughts of where and how I could get alcohol. Without it I felt physically sick, often vomiting, with hot and cold sweats, and uncontrollable shaking. I felt jittery and anxious, almost panicking and I would be unable to calm myself down. With just one drink, all of these symptoms would disappear.

During my last two years of drinking I was permanently afraid. I was afraid of being alone and yet I wanted to be on my own. I was afraid of dying but every morning I woke up, I was afraid of having to live another day. I was afraid that alcohol was going to kill me, but I was more afraid of trying to live without it. I was afraid that I would accidently over-dose and my body would not be discovered for weeks or months later. I was afraid of what this would do to my Mum and to my family.

Finally, I started to comprehend the wreckage of my life. I realised that my drinking and drug use not only exacerbated all my existing problems, it actually created entirely new ones, but the prospect of changing was terrifying. I would have to deal with giving up the one thing that, no matter what its physical or emotional toll, afforded me a reprieve from the pain. I felt scared and desperate. My despair made me feel like I was drowning but if I could summon the courage to reach out there was a glimmer of hope. That hope was Mum and my family.

In moments of clarity I knew deep down, that my family would be there for me. I made a phone-call to my sister, Cathy and told her about the dire straits I was in. I told her of my fears and my need to be at home. She reassured me and told me that my family would help me.

Early the following morning, my eldest brother Keith was banging on my flat door in the Elephant & Castle. Without accusation or judgement, he simply said, "I've come to bring you home".

It did not take me long to pack. After more than 20 years in London, I was returning to Ireland with my entire life in 2 black refuse sacks and my dog Sasha by my side. After locking the door for the last time, I realised that I had only one person to tell that I was leaving and that was Gerry. I had not seen him for quite some time, but we spoke occasionally on the phone. I did not want him to see just how hopeless I had become so I cowardly rang him to say 'goodbye'.

Sitting in the front seat of Keith's car as we travelled to Holyhead my mind was in turmoil. I was relieved that the life I had been living was coming to end, but I was terrified of what lay ahead of me. I was so looking forward to seeing Mum and the rest of my family, but I became swamped with feelings of shame at the thought of having to explain to them the kind of person I had become. I realised that the phone call I had made to Cathy was an act of surrender on my part. I was so desperate and depressed that I had willingly relinquished myself to the loving care of my family and so I would now have to gratefully accept their support in whatever it was going to take for me to turn my life around.

After boarding the boat in Holyhead, I realised that I would not be able to make the journey without a drink. I had already become very anxious and my hands had started to shake. I could feel my heart beating rapidly and knew that I had to get a drink. I bought a small bottle of vodka in the duty-free shop and locked myself into a cubicle in the Ladies toilet to drink it. With the first swallow there was an instant sensation of euphoria and relief, but this was quickly followed by intense feelings of shame and revulsion.

When I thought about my family's immediate reaction to my plea for help, I was disgusted by own inability to help myself. I knew that I had to be honest, with them and with myself so I decided to tell Keith straight away what I had done. His initial response was anger.

"What the hell am I supposed to do now?" he asked.

"You can't land home drunk! What would Mum say?"

I felt overwhelming shame.

When I pictured Mum standing at the door of our family home, I was so happy, but I also had a huge sense of guilt. I thought of how disappointed she would be in me. But I knew that feeling ashamed and guilty would not help. I had to start taking responsibility for my own well-being.

"Would you ring Michelle? Ask her if she can get me an appointment with a doctor as soon as she can. If I get a prescription for something it would help me over the worst of it", I suggested.

"OK, I'll ring Michelle. I'll have to wait 'til we get into Dun Laoghaire though. I've no signal on my phone out here in the middle of the Irish Sea".

When we arrived at the house on the Rock late that evening, Mum came running out to meet us.

"You're going to be ok now that you're home", she said to me.

"Look at the cut of you, you're nothing but skin and

bone. Good job I've the stew on".

I laughed and cried at the same time. The pot of stew was always Mum's welcome gesture for all of us whenever we would be coming home.

"Did you put carrots in it?" I asked jokingly.

"I did. You can't make stew without carrots. But I can pick them out if you still don't like them".

"It's good to be home, Mum", I said.

It was only then that Mum noticed Sasha, although she was hard to miss with all the barking she was doing.

"Yes, you can have a bit of stew too", Mum said as she bent down to pat Sasha's head.

With that Sasha went running into the house ahead of us, as though to take her up on her offer before she changed her mind.

"Hey Arl", Michelle said when I walked in. "Keith was telling us the craic. Whenever you are ready, I have the telephone number for the 'out of hours' doctor".

I rushed to give her a big hug. "Thanks sis", I muttered.

Michelle has always been the 'go to person' in the family for getting things done. Even though she is younger than me she took charge of looking after me as though I was the younger one and I knew that I was in very good hands. As we sat in the doctor's waiting room later that evening, she took hold of my hand and said, "don't worry, it'll be ok. Whatever happens we'll do it as a family".

We were brought up to value family and as a result we have always been very close. Since Dad died, I think it became even more important for us all to look out for one another and without that, I knew that I would have died alone and afraid in a flat in London. My name was called and we both walked in to see the doctor.

Telling him why I was there was difficult because I felt so ashamed. His behaviour towards me added to my humiliation as he, in no uncertain terms instructed me to take one Librium every day for a week and to attend regular AA meetings if I had any true intentions of stopping drinking. With that he handed me a prescription and called for the next patient through the intercom. I was mortified. Michelle was livid.

"Who does he think he is? Could just as easy be a member of his family with a drink problem!" she said angrily as we made our way back home.

"Is he the usual doctor?" I asked.

"No thank God!" she answered.

"I don't know him at all. He's obviously a locum filling in. We won't be asking for him again".

"We won't need to go through that again", I said optimistically.

I was so grateful to be living back at home, but I did not envisage how difficult it would be. Mum was fantastic and even though mine and Sasha's sudden arrival created a massive change to her life she never made me feel as though we were infringing on her. In fact, it was quite the opposite. She constantly commented on how great it was to have someone to light the fire, a task she readily admitted to never having successfully conquered in her many years of trying. She was also delighted that Sasha and her dog, Saimie got on so well together and she loved putting on her wellies to take them both up over the fields opposite the house for a runabout.

But I was really struggling with adapting to the changes to my life. I could not settle back to living in a small town after living so long in the city. I felt as though I was always on the brink of something, waiting for something to happen that would give me a reason to be there. Other than fighting with the demons inside me and trying not to drink I had no motivation to even think about what I was going to do. I had no purpose, aims or long-term goals.

The demons that I was in constant battle with were the flashbacks of abuse and pain. Almost every room in my family home held a nightmare.

Each time I walked into the front bedroom I could see Mum holding Siobhán's limp little body and I heard my own voice screaming for her to wake her up. The old rolled up grey blanket that was once tightly tucked up against the bottom of the back door was now replaced with a proper draught excluder but I felt its dampness beneath me, a grown man on top of me every time I walked into the narrow scullery to make a cup of tea. The guns on the wall were long gone, put away for safe keeping as heirlooms in memory of Dad but even the now empty wall held fear for me as I heard the threat of the abuser so long ago.

Going outside the house was just as fearful as I was constantly on alert for the appearance of an abuser. I was terrified about what might happen should I come face to face with someone from my past, just as I had done in London. I scanned the streets as I walked from A to B and breathed a sigh of relief every time I made it home safely. My mind was in constant chaos, running through a variety of different scenarios and possible outcomes and through it all I kept silent, putting on an act just as I had always done.

The only way that I knew how to cope with what was going on inside my head was to drink or to use drugs. I knew that Mum would be horrified if she realised that I had been a drug user, but I could convince myself and her that a couple of beers would do no harm.

On one of her treks out with the dogs she returned to find me sitting on the front doorstep drinking a can of lager. At first, she was stunned, then angry and probably afraid.

"What are you doing drinking?" she asked.

By this time, I had myself fully convinced that I could be a normal drinker and for quite a while after that it appeared as though I was.

"It's only a beer Mum. I bought 2 and the other one is still in the fridge. Have it if you fancy it", I said sounding very confident.

She walked pass me into the house saying, "I don't like beer but that doesn't mean that you have to drink it!"

"There's no need to worry Mum", I said reassuringly. "I have no intention of drinking anything other than a beer or two from now on. I promise".

Of course, I knew that she would be worried, and I felt so guilty for that, but I knew that I would never manage what was going on for me without having the safety net of a drink. The rest of the family were also very concerned when they knew that I was drinking again but over the following few months their concerns lessened. They could see for themselves that I was holding to my promise of only having a couple of beers, now and again.

For the first time in quite a while the spotlight was well and truly off me when Michelle and her husband, Dave announced that they were expecting a baby. It was exciting news and I did whatever I could to help prepare for the new arrival to the family. It was my opportunity to finally be able to do something worthwhile to help. I went shopping for creams and nappies and other baby things with Michelle but stayed out of the way when the expectant mum and dad wanted to buy the bigger things like a cot and a pram together. When Dave asked me to help him to paint the nursery, I felt that I was a part of something very special.

On 28th October 2004 Grace was born. The I first time I saw her my heart did a jolt, I instantly loved her. It was such an emotional experience that I knew that this tiny person was going to be a major feature in my life. When Michelle and Dave brought her home, I volunteered to look after her when they needed a break for an hour or two. She never made shy with me and I think this was because she sensed, in whatever way babies do, how much I loved her.

When she was a little older, I introduced her to Sasha. Sasha's behaviour around her was extraordinary. She would sit by the cot when Grace was asleep as though she was on guard duty and would not leave until the baby awoke again. When I took Grace out for a walk Sasha would walk alongside the pram and nothing would distract her from her task.

Over the following months Grace became the most important part of my life and thankfully Michelle and Dave were very supportive of that. I felt, for the first time in a very long time that I could be worthwhile and of value again.

However, as much as I tried, I could not feel that way all of the time. I still struggled with so many unresolved issues and my feelings around that contradicted so strongly how I felt about myself when I was with Grace. Just as I had done when I was a child, I separated these two parts of myself. When I was with Grace, I completely disassociated from all the negative emotions of my childhood and detached from the pain of losing Siobhán in order to fully participate in the joy of loving Grace but when I was alone, I was a wreck.

207

The intrusive thoughts and images that I could evade when I was with Grace would overwhelm me when I was by myself and the feelings of shame and guilt that I was able to suppress would engulf and overpower me.

I resorted to my usual coping method, alcohol. Rather than drinking only a couple of beers every now and again I progressed to 5 or 6 every few days. For some time that amount allowed me to manage when I was struggling and gave me the sober space to be with Grace on the days when I was not drinking.

The beginning of the progression was relatively slow but evident none the less. I was back to lying about how much and how often I was drinking. As well as that I was drinking spirits but denied it when anyone questioned me. I continued to insist that I was only 'having a few beers' and that everything was fine. Whether anyone believed me or not never seemed to have crossed my mind.

I was also back to having blackouts every time I drank. Days and nights vanished just as they had before. I would be terrified sobering up after a blackout because I would have had no idea about what I had done. If nobody offered to enlighten me, I would be so relieved and this, in my messed-up way of thinking, gave me the freedom to drink again. By the time Grace was nearing a year old I was living on a day to day basis, sometimes less than that. On the days that I planned to visit her I was sober but by that night, I would be drinking. My visits became less frequent and after some time I finally realised that I was spending more time drinking than I was with Grace.

I was back to where I had been, lost and desperate with my addiction. At times I thought of reaching out to my family again, but I felt too ashamed to ask them for help a second time. I had let them down so badly. If they chose to wash their hands of me, I would not blame them.

But deep down I knew that that would not be the case. I had allowed myself to believe that my family would turn their backs on me just so I could continue to drink and wallow in the pain of my past. One morning I plucked up the courage and rang Michelle.

"Hey Shell", I said.

"Hi sis. What you up to?" she asked.

I jumped straight in.

"Shell, will you bring me to the doctor? I want to stop drinking."

"Give me half an hour to sort Grace out and I'll be there".

She hung up before I could say anything else.

I sat down on the floor and cried. I stayed there until she arrived.

"We have an appointment in 20 minutes", she said. "Hopefully its not the same bollox that we got last time".

"I don't care who we get. I'll tell him that I want to go into the hospital this time because I just know that I can't do it on my own with one week of tablets".

"Don't worry about that yet" she said.

"Let's just wait 'till we get there. Come on, get in the car. We don't want to be late".

My experience with Doctor Raymond Kerr was something very different to the one I had with the other doctor. I had prepared myself to be questioned, judged and sentenced to 14 days in a *'drying out'* ward. I could not have been more wrong.

As soon as we entered the room, Doctor Kerr turned away from his desk and invited me to sit in one of the chairs opposite him. He held my hand as he spoke and although I felt like I was the lowest piece of scum ever discovered on this planet or on any other, he treated me with kindness, dignity and even respect.

He said the words that I have never forgotten..."today is the first day of the rest of your life!"

At the time I had little understanding of what that phrase really meant but it had been seared into my mind and became a very profound and reflective statement that I would continually fall back on for motivation and support.

I knew that this encounter was the first real step to fully committing to a future free of alcohol and drugs.

"Will you go into the hospital Arylene?", Doctor Kerr asked.

"Yes, I will doctor. I'll do whatever you think is best".

As I was speaking, I could see Michelle in my peripheral vision as she sat beside me. She was shaking her head indicating her disapproval of this suggestion.

When I turned to look at her, she said, "is there any other way doctor? We don't want her going into the mental hospital. Can we look after her at home if you give her something?"

In a very gentle manner doctor Kerr said, "No, no. I didn't mean the psychiatric hospital. I meant Sligo General. Alcohol withdrawal can be complicated, and it would be better to do it under medical supervision, especially given that Arylene has epilepsy. Is that ok?"

"When will I go?" I asked.

"Right away. I'll ring to say that you are on your way", he replied as he lifted the phone.

"We'll stop at the house to tell Mum and get the things you'll need for now. Then we'll head off", Michelle said.

When we arrived at the hospital, we were told that there was a bed waiting for me on the female medical ward. I was immediately put into a gown and a canula was put into my arm to connect me up to a drip hanging above the top of the bed. Another canula was inserted into the back of my hand which I was told would be used whenever they needed to give me medication. While this was going on a nurse was drawing blood into a number of vials and depositing them into a kidney dish sitting on the trolly that she had brought with her. Another nurse was sticking the plastic discs to my chest which I knew would be connected to a heart monitor.

Within an hour of our arrival a doctor came to speak with me. Her manner was kind though honest.

"Miss Murphy, you are here to undergo an alcohol and drug detoxification".

I was not sure if this was a question or a statement, so I did not answer.

"We are aware that you have epilepsy, but you also have malnutrition and possibly a number of other medical issues. But don't worry, we'll look after you".

"Thank you, doctor", I muttered shamefully.

The following 10 days were mostly a blur. However, the hallucinations as a result of delirium tremens (DT's) were memorable and terrifying. I believed that I could see ants crawling under my skin and I scratched and tore at my legs and arms trying to get them out. I also saw lizards running across the ward floor and hiding under the curtains pulled around another patient's bed. What frightened me most was the image of a tribe of Zulu warriors surrounding my bed, each holding a long spear with a human head fixed on top. One of the heads was mine.

When I started to feel better, I thought about what my next step would be. Although I did not want to drink or use drugs again, I was afraid that once I got out of the hospital, I would not be able to stay clean and sober.

I knew that I was using alcohol and drugs in an attempt to distance myself from all the pain and loss in my life especially about where all that pain began, the sexual abuse I experienced as a child and I was terrified that once the crutch was removed, I would not be able to cope.

When the time came for me to be dis-charged from the hospital I told my doctor of my fears.

"That's exactly what I've come to speak to you about", she said.

"If you agree I can refer you to a residential treatment centre. You would be there for 5 weeks and they do a 2 year follow up programme. I think it would give you the best chance of staying healthy".

"Sounds expensive. I don't have a penny to my name".

It felt like I was being offered a lifeline while at the same time it was being yanked away from me.

"This place does accept people with a medical card, in which case it would cost you nothing. However, that might involve going on a waiting list. If you are genuinely interested in giving this 100% effort, I can make you an urgent referral, but that may or may not speed things up. I would rather refer you directly from hospital if that were possible. That would mean you'd have to pay. Could your family help?"

"I don't know. I'd feel awful asking them" I replied.

"It's up to you. We can keep you here for another day or

212

two but after that we'll need the bed. Let me know what you want to do", she said as she walked away.

I knew what I wanted to do. I really wanted to go to rehab.

That night Mum, Cathy, Padraig, Michelle and Dave, came to visit me. They were delighted to see how well I was doing and asked when I might be getting home. It was decided that Sasha and I would stay with Mum for as long as I needed to get back on my feet so there was no need to worry about looking for work or a place to live for a while yet. When visiting time was over, I asked Michelle to stay behind for a quick word. I told her about what the doctor had said.

"What's the name of the place that she wants you to go?", she asked.

"White Oaks Treatment Centre. It's in Donegal", I answered as I handed her the pamphlet the doctor left.

"Never heard of it but I'll find out. Don't worry about it. We'll sort something out", she said as she hugged me 'goodbye'.

The doctor came to see me again the following morning to tell me that she could refer me to the treatment centre that day.

"Your sister rang this morning to say that the cost of your treatment has been arranged. I have already telephoned White Oaks and they have a bed available. It's up to you now. Do you want to go?"

I was stunned. It was all happening so fast. But I was in no doubt.

"Yes, I want to go as soon as possible", I said with enthusiasm tinged with a slight hint of apprehension.

"They are expecting you this afternoon. Can your family

213

bring you?"

"I'll ring home but I'm sure they will".

Within 3 hours Mum and I were sitting in the back seat of Dave's car while Michelle sat in the front passenger seat armed with a road map to offer directions to White Oaks. As we made our way out of Sligo towards Donegal my apprehension grew.

"Do you know where this place is Shell?" I asked.

"Not a clue", she replied.

"But if we get lost, we can phone the place. It's well signposted apparently so we'll get there one way or another".

Throughout the journey it felt as though we were on a family day out and not on our way to an addiction rehab centre. We spoke about mundane things which made the long road trip more tolerable. As we neared our destination, I began to feel more and more anxious though not enough to want to turn back. I knew that this was the next step to my getting well and I was determined to take it.

After taking a few wrong turns in the middle of nowhere and then doubling back we finally arrived at a building situated somewhere between the Donegal and Derry border. We were all invited in and ushered into, what looked like a sitting room. It struck me that I was surprised to find the place more homely than clinical. For some reason I assumed that it would be more like a hospital even though my experience of rehab centres was zero.

Within minutes a woman came in and sat with us. She asked me a series of questions about myself and filled in some paperwork with my replies. She then said that I could have time to say goodbye to my family and she would return in a while to bring me to my room.

"If you don't like it you can come home", Mum said.

"Don't be telling her that!", Michelle retorted.

"It's rehab, I don't think you're meant to like it!"

Everyone started to laugh which made the parting easier for all of us, though I would have thought if anyone outside the room had heard us, they would assume we were all crazy.

The thought of staying 5 weeks in a place where I had no notion of what was going to happen to me was initially very daunting but meeting the other residents instantly lessened my fears. I think this was because we were all there for the same reason and we shared a sense of commonality. That feeling of *togetherness* deepened as time went on probably because in group therapy, we shared parts of ourselves that we would never have shared before. We could identify with one another and talk about how our addictions had damaged our lives and destroyed our dreams.

The most painful things that I could not have shared in group I shared with Mae, my roommate. Mae's life was so different to mine, yet we had so much in common. We both endured losses and we both found solace in the bottle. We both struggled and we both sought peace and recovery. In White Oaks we laughed, and we cried together, we held each other up when we were having a tough day and we shared our learning to boost each other on. Somehow, I just knew that Mae and I were destined to be friends long after rehab.

Family Day was the hardest day for all of us and we dreaded its arrival like a scourge. This weekly event involved members of our families coming in to share their experience of how our addictions had impacted on their lives as well as what they hoped the future for everyone would be. Hearing their pain was very often more difficult to bear than our own.

My Mum told me about her fear of standing by her

daughter's graveside and Cathy said she wanted her big sister back. Keith and Gavin were angry that I was throwing my life away and Padraig said he just wanted a chance to get to know me. Dave jokingly said that he wanted a babysitter for Grace, but it was what Michelle said that really hit home.

"Arl, we can't let you be around Grace if you are drinking. What if something happened and she got hurt?"

My heart felt like it had exploded inside my body when I realised that I could hurt Grace because of my drinking. From the very second that Michelle mentioned her name, something inside me shifted and I knew that I would never drink or use drugs again. Although I did not fully understand how this epiphany had come about, I felt it, deep down somewhere in my soul that something life-changing had happened.

For the first time since arriving in White Oaks I allowed myself to think about what had happened to Siobhán and the part my drinking had played. For the past month my counsellor Denyse had been trying to encourage me to talk about the night Siobhán died but I consistently refused. I completely shut down whenever she or anyone else tried to get me to talk about it.

When Mae and I were having our last smoke before bed that night, I told her the whole story. I knew that she would not judge me nor condemn me. She listened as I spoke about how, as a result of a blackout, I lost the last precious hours that I could have shared with my baby girl. Mae held me as I rocked, my body heaving as I cried for the first time with sober tears. Then she too cried for her baby boy, and we comforted each other, 2 mothers heartbroken for the children they had lost.

Finally, Mae said, in her beautiful Derry accent, "you'll

be ok to talk to Denyse now Arylene. When you talk to her about Siobhán, make sure you tell her about Grace. Tell her how much Grace means to you. I don't know why but I think that's important".

Mae was right. My recovery is about healing from the past and living freely in the present.

Grace has been the instigation of my freedom. Not only my freedom from addiction but from the pain and the loss that fuelled my addiction. She opened the doors that I was afraid to open and gave me the strength to walk through them.

Chapter 12

A vital part of White Oak's recovery programme was that sobriety could only be achieved if we truly believed that we were doing it for our own benefit and not for someone else's. Up to that point I struggled to find a real reason for my living never mind a true reason for getting into recovery from addiction. Even my decision to come home from London was because I did not want my Mum to suffer the pain and loss of my being found dead from an overdose of alcohol and drugs.

I fully accepted what my family wanted, not just for themselves but for me, yet I could not get past the feelings of worthlessness and loathing that I had internalised for as long as I could remember. Although I did want my life to be different, I could not find any real purpose, that was solely beneficial to me, for changing it.

Until now.

Grace has given me purpose. Being a part of her life gave me a reason to live for me. I wanted to be someone important to her and someone that she would be happy to be around as she got older. I wanted to be someone that she would talk to when there was something going on in her life. I just wanted to be able to be there for her as she was growing up, one of the many supportive adults around her. I wanted her to love me and be proud of who I was going to become.

When the residential part of the treatment programme ended, the 2-year aftercare programme began. This involved returning to White Oaks one evening a week for on-going support as we made the adjustment to a new way of living. I also attended weekly one to one counselling sessions for the first 11 months in order to heal from the traumas I had survived throughout my life.

When I initially spoke about the sexual abuse in my childhood it was simply as a detailed account of a series of events. I did not feel any of it, I was afraid to. I was afraid of the years of mounting pain and I was afraid of letting it all go in case it swallowed me up.

For so long I had to keep my feelings locked inside and to suppress the pain. This was my way of protecting myself. At the time this defence method shielded me from awareness and allowed me to function.

Over my years of drinking and drugging I had cut myself off from other people as well as from myself and my feelings. I had isolated myself not only on a physical level but on an emotional one. Because of this I had great difficulty with relationships. I found it impossible to trust anyone, especially with my feelings. Once I had stopped drinking and using drugs my only method of surviving was the way I had learned as a child, to be silent.

It was second nature to me to lay down ways of avoiding my deepest hurts –I'd had years of practice. While always respecting and emphasizing my ability to make my own choices my counsellor carefully and gently offered alternatives to every obstacle that I put in my own path.

Slowly but eventually I began to feel safe. Learning to trust another person, was a monumental step in my recovery. Creating a safe and trusting environment enabled me to accept my past and to recognise the feelings associated with it.

For almost a year I worked hard to untie the damaging thoughts that I had believed and carried throughout my life. These thoughts had become my personal beliefs about myself, every one of them damning and critical. Some days were more difficult than others, but I knew that I wanted to stay on this road of recovery which meant that any possibility of relapsing back into the world of addiction could not be deemed an option. The ongoing surveillance and support of the White Oaks aftercare programme ensured that I could manage the deepest painful feelings and heal from the devastating impact of the traumas I had survived.

After completing my 2-year aftercare treatment programme White Oaks asked me to train as a group facilitator, an honour that was to be another poignant and influential step in my exhilarating journey. I spent 4 years as a volunteer with White Oaks and it was during this time that I developed the confidence to consider working with other people who were struggling with some of the issues that I had struggled with.

I began my career by achieving a Diploma in Addictions through the University of Limerick and under the guidance of White Oak's most experienced counsellor, Majella Coyle, I was accepted by the University of Ulster to train as a Psychotherapist.

Majella became my supervisor in my training and with her direction I graduated with a distinction in my degree. These academic accomplishments were, in themselves, proof of the miracle of recovery but beyond that, to the phenomenon of how a person who was once so lost, so down and so discarded could achieve so much.

I now have the very special privilege of being a part of the journey of others who are struggling to see that there is joy in life after childhood sexual abuse and addiction. I believe that my own personal experiences with trying to simply survive as an adult allows me to empathize with another abuse survivor on a level that only they are aware of and for me that is an exceptional gift.

My personal experience has given me an insight into what someone seeking help hopes to find and that is first and foremost, a trusting and caring listener.

As a client myself once and now as a counsellor I believe that the trust within a counselling relationship is the most powerful element to achieving freedom from the trauma of abuse.

It is within that trusting and safe environment that both my client and I work together to develop a deeper understanding of what has happened to them and how they have survived it. Through this process my clients come to know that they are no longer victims, but survivors, in charge of their own lives. They recognise their strengths and their abilities to bring about positive changes so that they can become the person that they choose to be.

Through my work and my constant learning, I continue to gain further insight into the devastating impact of sexual abuse and other childhood traumas. I have come to know that trauma is not simply about a particular event, it is more about how we respond to that adverse event, how we have experienced it, not just when it happened but for many years after.

Being sexually abused as a child impacted me in many ways and for a very long time, I would have been unaware of most of them. Behaviours that I developed at the time in response to the trauma, for example how I was always on guard, afraid that something awful was going to happen to me continued into my adulthood. Years after the abuse ended, I remained hypervigilant, anxious and fearful of the world and the people in it. I struggled to make real connections with friends when I was younger and as an adult, I had great difficulties with relationships. Unwanted memories and flashbacks from my childhood would come to mind incessantly leaving me feeling worthless and ashamed just as I did as a child. The constant replay of the abuse felt like I was re-experiencing it and being re-traumatised by it, years later.

Most of the time, being inside my own head was a very frightening and painful place to be. Using alcohol and drugs allowed me space from that. My addictions helped to suppress the intrusive memories and made the hypervigilance more manageable. For as long as I could remember I felt worthless, hopeless and broken. The self-destructiveness of addiction made me feel like I was living in alignment with who I was. In a mind that had been injured by trauma I thought that using substances, even to the detrimental amount that I had been using, was my choice and within my control. This helped to reinstate the choice and control that had been taken from me as a child.

In other words, I used alcohol and drugs to self-medicate. Using these substances eased the debilitating painful symptoms of my unresolved traumas. In fact, addiction helped me to survive. Although the use of substances is obviously a negative response, it is not an uncommon one for adult survivors of childhood trauma.

For the first 41 years of my life I was a victim. My path had been pre-determined by the sexual abuse I endured in my childhood. I believe that recovery from my addiction would have been impossible if the trauma was left unresolved. When the issues that led to the addiction were addressed and healed, then the need to self-medicate was removed.

Today I am who I choose to be, and I can do that because my family never gave up on me. Without their continuous love and support I would not be able to be the person I am or to do the work I do.

Grace is and will always be the most important person in my life. She is my inspiration, my motivation, my purpose and my power. She is my second chance at living, and at loving. I love her as my own daughter, in fact Michelle and Dave have given me the honour of being legally recognised as her 3rd parent. I have chosen to accept that honour and embrace the joy that comes with it.

Carl Jung famously said,

"I am not what happened to me. I am who I choose to be".

I totally agree!!!